THIRD WORLD WOMAN

WEIRD AF TALES OF AN ACCIDENTAL FEMINIST

SHAHLA KHAN

Contents

This book is dedicated to you, my reader

A woman's rights never come served on a plate like strawberries and cream.

Nor like a gift with a pretty bow on top.

A woman has always had to fight for her rights.

To snatch them forcibly from the unwilling guardians of culture, tradition and political empires.

Some snatch those rights successfully; some die trying; and the rest are too busy feeding the patriarchs to see the ornamental leashes on their necks and feet.

I wish you success in your battle for your right to a free, independent and deserving life.

Your fellow warrior,

Shahla

Preface

———⚜———

You know what sucks?

Life when under the control of others. That sucky life is unfortunately a dark reality for millions of people and in this book I tried to capture some parts of that suckiness. This book is simultaneously the most enjoyable and challenging project that I have undertaken in quite some time. Once you have finished reading I am sure that you, my dear reader, will feel the same.

Third World Woman is a collection of 'weird-as-fuck' stories, essays and observations, collated over several years. Growing up as a woman of colour in a third world country, then juggling the cultural contradictions of modern life in the UK, has rarely been anything less than interesting.

Within these pages, you'll find stories of incidents that happened to myself, and the women that I grew up with and around. Some of these will make you laugh until you pee your pants, and others will make you hate the guts of certain people. Others still may compel you to think deeper about the ways you perceive life, while some may go as far as to change your life altogether.

I feel as though I am completing the task I was sent to planet Earth for by writing and sharing this book with you. This is because I have a very unique set of experience, carrying three distinct labels – Indian, Muslim, and Feminist.

Being Indian comes with a lot of cultural baggage, and blending it with Islamic values is a whole new angle on life. When you add 'feminism' to that, the magic happens. Suddenly, the chaotic mushy pumpkin turns into a beautiful, sexy and stylish carriage of life for me – the Cinderella of this story! Except, I'm nothing like Cinderella. More like an Indian Gloria Steinem, trapped in the body of Merida. Only 6 sizes bigger, and caramel brown in skin tone.

It's not all about me, though; it's about the lives of women in third world countries. The stories you'll read in this book are all real-life accounts of living, breathing human beings. Although many women will relate to these experiences, it would be far-sighted to claim that all women face this life. The fact is, I am an educated woman who had the opportunity to study and travel the world on my own, develop my own opinions, read, and live an independent life. These are just some of the privileges that many of us take for granted.

Many women in third world countries do not go to school. Many of them do not even have access to safe drinking water or sanitation. There are villages in India where men marry twice or thrice, just to fetch water from a far away well – Google the term Water Wives for the details. Those that do receive an education come from different classes and income backgrounds, which plays a prominent role in their lives. Not all women grow up in families with the same superstitions and values.

Now, there is a special message that I'd like to tell you about men; there are both good and bad men out there. The stories of this book are about the ones that shock me and chill me to my bones, but this in no way should be taken that I hate all men, or that I'd claim there are no good men at all. So, allow me to address the #NotAllMen brigade right here with a simple message – cool your jets. We *know* #NotAllMen, because hey, my own dad is one of those male beings..

The fact is, men started feminism in India, sort of. Granted, they *had* to because women did not have the appropriate standing in society to begin with, but the point stands; men are capable of using their influence for either good or evil. This book will talk about certain stories, based on experiences – it is not a debate or discussion platform where I might be expected to present a balanced view. This isn't a Men vs. Women battle of the sexes. It's literally a first-hand account of a third world woman who has witnessed many strange things in her life. Along the way she realised how big of a feminist she has always been, but only recently discovered the appropriate terminology to announce this fact.

As I write, I want you to know what a weird position I'm in. I am privileged and oppressed at the same time. The thing is, it's not just gender; there are many other factors that play an important role that shape our experiences. In the third world, your race, class, religion and abilities play a huge role, too. You know what wins in the long term? Wealth!

The famous actor Salman Khan is one such example. Westerners who are unfamiliar with the name, Google is your friend. Women in wealthy families can beat, humiliate and injure the men and women who work as domestic servants for them.

Women in the third world have got a bad deal, but the position men find themselves in is frequently little better. It's silly to compare numbers and fight for just one side because the truth is, it's a messed up world out there, and those with the deepest pockets win. Granted, these are often men, since they hold the financial resources and inherit family wealth.

My own privilege is that I grew up the daughter of diplomat, a man that believed in educating his children to conquer the world. I have travelled to Europe independently, which is almost unheard of in my entire extended family and neighbourhood. I have lived many great experiences, and since my family isn't *super*-conservative, I have enjoyed a better quality of life than many others. This is why I'm using my privilege to write this book, and share the true picture with the world.

But what is the other side of the picture? Is it as great as it superficially appears? What did I have to go through, and what dilemmas do I still encounter when I visit home? Why does my mother still feel that she is under a curse because I'm single, despite having supported myself without family help for last seven years? What kind of societal pressures try to break down my spine? What does it take to escape an arranged marriage?

Most importantly; how well does a white person know and understand a brown woman?

This is important, because we are almost everywhere. The sooner you get to know brown women, the better it will be. Humanity will progress, businesses will thrive, and expensive, potentially bankrupting lawsuits can be avoided.

This book is a peek into the third world situation of my life and those around me, first hand.

Chapter 1

Congratulations! It's a... FEMINIST?

"Humour is a way of saying something very serious sometimes. This is my attempt at it."

I'm weird. That's not me being self-deprecating; it's just what I have been told. That's because people are never more comfortable than when applying labels, and I am a strange combination of three of those convenient tags that often make for uneasy bedfellows; Indian, Muslim and Feminist

The Indian label is God-given, as He provided my birth within in an Indian family.

The Muslim label is a gift of my parents, who raised me with Islamic values.

The third label is bestowed upon me by myself, and the story of how that came to be will be discussed in this chapter.

I largely enjoy all three of my labels, but somehow they don't fit together too well. For instance, the Indian label conflicts with its feminist counterpart, as most Indians believe in orthodox traditions. The Muslim tag is fighting against both Indian and feminist labels, since a Muslim woman is one with hijab and never attends a co-ed school in a country like India (atleast the stereotype of one is). I'm a masterpiece of imperfections. The imperfect Indian, the unconventional Muslim, and the modern feminist.

Sadly we live in a world of strong stereotypes. We are expected to trim the edges of our ideology and squeeze ourselves within the parameters of hard cold boxes designed by society and held by tradition. If you're a square peg and you're faced with a round hole, that's unfortunate but it's down to you to make the best of a bad situation.

You are no longer you, but someone in a box. Just like when you buy a packet of Skittles, you know exactly what's inside. It makes things easier for the people on top. Hence, as humans, we are forced be trimmed and shoved into boxes of religion, culture and nationalities, making it easier to just look at the label and assume that we know the contents from the outside. We are like a Skittle hidden under an anonymous packet, with no colour and flavour of our own. Nobody ever opens the packet and asks whom you are – they don't need to. You are just a silly Skittle, designed to be hurled down the throat of a stranger and forgotten about.

And so, I thought, was I. Just a nameless tomato, squished alongside a million others, poured down into a Bolognaise bottle transported to a nameless distribution warehouse. A nameless intestine of a once-happy pig somewhere in the farms of nature, suddenly butchered by a factory machine, shaped into a bubblegum flavoured condom, and ending up on a purple penis of a man unwilling to use me. The condom, that is.

I was OK with this. Growing up, I never saw the big picture of these boxes, bottles and packets. I never realised that our branding and packaging was constantly completed without me even *noticing* any of it. All I knew was I came in an Indian box, with a Muslim stamp across the lid.

One fine day, a usually unremarkable incident occurred that was the beginning of my third label. I became a *female*. Earlier, I was told that I was a child. Suddenly, I became a female child. This was a bit confusing over the years, because now I was not just that nameless tomato in the anonymous Bolognaise bottle, or the nameless intestine of that slaughtered pig. I was now the *female* tomato; the *female* intestine!

That realisation came with the onset of puberty, and several similar events took place over the years. With each awakening, the messages became more confusing. For instance, earlier I was given the message to, "study and work hard." Gradually the message changed into, "study but only so much that it could help you find a wealthy husband."

"Dream and think as much as you wish to" gradually evolved into, "dream about a happily married life, and think of all the sacrifices that lie ahead of you."

"Oh, that pink skirt! Your daughter looks so cute in it!" gradually changed to, "oh *my*! That pink skirt! Does your daughter not know how to dress appropriately?" as though the garments were one and the same from the ages of five and fifteen. Trust me, it was a different pink skirt!

The examples kept on coming. "We send you to school to study and learn, stay away from boys" transformed into, "why the hell don't you quit school and find a guy to marry? Get over this charade!"

"Wow, your daughter is so helpful to strangers – she has a big heart" turned into "wow, your daughter is an expert in finding excuses to loiter and gain attention." Between the lines that translated as "your daughter is a slut."

"Sweetie, you can be whoever you want to be" became, "Sweetie, you can be whoever your husband allows you to be."

I could go on, but I'm sure that you understand my point by now. At this stage of my development I was not even the nameless tomato; I was the useless stem that was tossed away the moment the tomato was ready to be squished. I was not the anonymous pig's equally anonymous intestine, but the toxic crap within that was to be washed and drained before the intestines could be used.

My purpose was only limited to hold and nurture the flower, and connect it to the roots for nourishment until the tomato was ready to go out into the unknown world on its own. Similar was my role in the pig's intestine; the nourishment inside the intestine was absorbed into the walls, and I was left inside like crap waiting to be excreted out. *I was the faeces*. That's not a good self-image for any young woman, let me tell you.

My life and purpose grew even shorter and increasingly mundane. There was so much more I could do and be; yet I was forever finding myself limited by *someone*. I was constantly reminded of my boundaries, and even if I did show my potential, it wasn't accepted. It wasn't good enough, and ultimately I was told to get back and not forget my place in this world.

I struggled to accept the identity that had been foisted upon me. I quibbled over the changing messages. I grumbled over the potential I had that went unrecognised. I could do a lot more than laundry and cooking, but somehow it just was so invisible to others. My worth was based on my weight and aesthetics. So if I still were a tomato, I just had to look plum and bright on the outside even if I was full of *Manduca quinquemaculata* (scientific name for tomato long worms, but you didn't need me to tell you that. You're obviously smart or you wouldn't have made the choice to purchase this book.) And if I were that infernal pig intestine, I just had to be inside a bouncing, hopping pig – even if I had cancerous cells throughout my length.

This disturbed me even more. I was repeatedly primed about the idea that what lies on the inside is useless, while what lies on the outside is worthy.

One day I could not take it any longer, and I announced my rebellion. Instantly I was asked if I were a 'feminist'; the third label. As a young girl, struggling with finances and unwilling to marry for money, I never knew what that word meant. Hence I began the exploration that would change my life.

Feminism told me that I was neither the stem nor the tomato. Neither was I the intestine, nor the crap it contained. I was *me*. A human like anyone else, but not confined to *doing* what everybody else did. Feminist is a label in itself, and there are assumptions related to this label just like the others. Despite this, it was far better than any alternative I had come across in a long time. And best of all, owning this label did not mean I had to renounce my previous brandings. Hence, I decided to own all three of these – Indian, Muslim and Feminist.

As a feminist, I didn't have to hate men, but to call out those who oppress women and children.

I didn't have to look ugly and unshaven, but to help people create a positive body image and love the blessing of limbs and healthy organs.

I didn't have to get unborn babies aborted, but to help women access proper healthcare so that babies come into welcoming homes with enough food and heat.

I didn't have to become immodest, but to help people realise that the only person with any ownership over their own sexuality was themselves.

Most importantly, I came out of that bubble world that was built around me by society and school. I could see that I was *not* the centre of the universe, and there were bigger problems in the world than deciding whether I was the stem or the fruit!

As Prügl lectured –

Violence against women can fit into several broad categories. These include violence carried out by 'individuals' as well as 'states.' Some of the forms of violence perpetrated by individuals are rape; domestic violence; sexual harassment; coercive use of contraceptives; female infanticide; prenatal sex selection; obstetric violence and mob violence; as well as harmful customary or traditional practices such as honour killings, dowry violence, female genital mutilation, marriage by abduction and forced marriage. Some forms of violence are perpetrated or condoned by the state such as war rape; sexual violence and sexual slavery during conflict; forced sterilization; forced abortion; violence by the police and authoritative personnel; stoning and flogging. Many forms of VAW, such as trafficking in women and forced prostitution are often perpetrated by organized criminal networks.

What started as a single identity struggle has now become a lifelong fight. My third label has made my first two more meaningful. It was that missing piece of the puzzle of me that gave meaning and purpose to my life. I now see the big picture of violence against women and connect it with my tiny piece, vowing to make changes through my existence. But I am also aware that monumental changes have glacial speed. What I *do* know, for now, is that I am that tiny drop in this substantial ocean that has created waves thrice already.

Today, I enjoy several privileges thanks to those women that bled and fought for my rights before, making this world a little easier to navigate for me and other women like me. As a result, I see it as my duty to lay these very same foundations for future generations.

The topmost section of Maslow's pyramid is self-actualization, described as,

"the realisation or fulfilment of one's talents and potentialities, especially considered as a drive or need present in everyone."

Embracing feminism helped me transform my entire life. This may seem an overstatement, or a big claim at first. How could a political ideology help someone transform her *personal* life?

Feminism taught me that I *mattered*, and that my gender is no excuse for anyone in the Goddamn world to oppress me. Not my family, not my friends, and not my husband or partner.

I started to work on myself, valuing my opinions while changing them as I educated myself on the issues of gender, race, class and identity. Basically, feminism helped me come out of the luxury bubble world I had been living in and identify my talents that I could use in order to make a difference in the world.

I was anti-gay. Frankly speaking (not speaking ill of Frank), I didn't even know homosexuality *existed* until I was 22. When I learned of this 'lifestyle', I was told it was all kinds of wrong, and as a result I hated the idea of it. Feminism educated me about homosexuality, and the fact that the human rights of LGBTQ individuals are every bit as important as any other human – what with them being human, and all. I'm an advocate now. This might seem trivial to a first world reader, but for somebody raised in a country where homosexuality is a criminal offence punishable by law, this change of mind was a bold step. Being ignorant about it is just not right.

I participated in slut shaming in my early twenties, because that is what we had been conditioned to do as young women. My mom would shame girls who would fail to dress according to her standards, and I learned that behaviour. As a result, not only would I repeat it, but I would blame victims when I came across assault stories.

I also had misconceptions about people of African origin, and white people in general – all of which were rooted in deep ignorance and self-righteousness. A general stereotype about white women back in the third world is that white women sleep with just anyone and everyone, and all black people are <insert an ignorant racist stereotype from the 1700s of your choosing here>. God, I have changed so much since I began learning about feminism.

The one thing I want to tell you if you identify as a feminist is that, nowadays, it's a cool label to pin to yourself. It's become a fashion statement for many people. Jennifer Lawrence is selling you a $710 shirt that says 'feminist', so *you too* can be in the mix of the movers and shakers. While embracing feminism is the best thing you will ever do for yourself, please take time to understand that feminism is *not* just a label; it's a responsibility.

If you call yourself a feminist, please invest time and energy in *educating yourself_*on the issues that are relevant to the everyday discussion. You do more harm than good if you claim to be a feminist and then disrespect a woman of colour, or a man of a different caste or sexual orientation.

Nobody can stop you from calling yourself any damn thing you wish, but I implore you to ensure you are a good – if not *excellent* – representative of what you claim to be.

Oh, and one last thing. A uterus is *not* mandatory to be a feminist.

That Kind of Girl

I am that kind of girl.

The girl who watches TED Talks. not cat videos

Maybe sleeps at 4am because she likes the world quiet.

The girl that eats what she likes, not what would make her small and take less space.

I am the kind of girl that will rip her heart out if you ask with love, and also the kind that will rip your tongue off if you demand it.

I am the kind that keeps a low profile in school.

Hangs out with everyone. Guys come to her for love advice and homework, but rarely to hit on her because her skirt is too long.

Few of those that hit on her would have lost their minds and probably became alcoholics because she rejected them.

I am the girl that doesn't know what bullying was cause she was too busy keeping her head down.

The girl in the corner of the playground with her pen, writing her dreams in her diary people called poetry.

I am the girl men admire from afar, but are too scared to get close because feminism!

They applaud the strong woman until she goes against their will and makes her choices.

Then, suddenly, she is selfish and insane and will die alone.

I am the girl too happy alone.

The girl with trust issues and her guard up all the time.

Hence my loneliness is my respite, and a safe place where I no more have to hide.

I am the girl that likes to dress up and put on make up.

Stare at the mirror and flirt with my reflection on car windows.

Who loves her body and face just the way it is.

I am that kind of girl that loves her Mom and Dad. No matter how far, no matter how distant.

The girl that saves her first penny and sends it straight to her Dad for his blessing.

The girl whose world begins and ends with the two people that she calls parents.

I am the kind of girl that doesn't like nationalities. Borders are drawn on maps and earth, but not on hearts.

Under the sky we are all one race and one kind. The girl that is neither patriotic nor religious, just kind enough to be called human.

Yes. I *am* that kind of girl.

Chapter 2

Being (Sub) Human , Humble beginnings, Misdemeanors and more

*W*hen I was a little girl, I wanted to be like a son my father never had.

When I grew up, I became the daughter no one in the freaking world had.

I guess, based on the surroundings, I thought (or rather was forced to think) that success and happiness was something only sons brought to the family. Daughters brought nothing but shame and financial burden, because sooner or later they would abandon the family for their husbands' one and never look back.

Selfish daughters.... yes there are many who are forced to end ties with their blood family, and many others use their blood family for money alone, showing loyalty instead to their in-laws where they are always treated as an outsider.

Being the second girl in the family was weird. Mom and Dad always loved us to the bones, but I remember the feeling of immense guilt built inside of me since early childhood. I would weep for my parents' pain that they had a second daughter when they could've had a son and been one big, happy family. There could be a little boy to hold my father's finger and stroll with him to the neighbourhood Masjid, where my father would flaunt his precious little son to other fathers who had been doing that to him. He would teach that little boy how to shave and build his muscles, to grow into a strong and powerful Khan. Instead they ended up with me; another daughter. A burden. I say this because there was nothing that I could give back to them for their love and care. A daughter is a weak piece of human flesh that just sucks all the money and attention, and one day disappears, never to return.

That's how *I* felt, but why did I feel this? My parents never said those things to me. They never told me not to dream or study. They never seemed disappointed with my performance or me. Honestly speaking, I don't remember *why* I felt that. Was it the movies? Was it the relatives back in India whom we visited once a year from Saudi Arabia? Was it the hidden messages in books that made me feel this way? Or maybe my parents *did* have a role to play in all of this, involuntarily, especially when we shifted to India.

We were sent to co-ed schools, but there were rules; we had to stay away from the boys. They could come home at times for homework or birthdays, but as I grew up it became a taboo since the people in my neighbourhood would talk smack about it and it started to bother my mom. I remember one incident in particular. Two of my male friends were home, and we were discussing something that had occurred in the classroom when mom barged in angrily and told them to get out and never return.

"What if your sisters had male friends who would come to your home and sit and chat in the living room for hours?" she asked. Mom's question touched a nerve for me, because it was true. The sisters of my male friends were not even allowed to *study* after 12th grade – forget about having male friends over for an after-school chat!

One thing that Indians have all wrong is the difference between an affair and a relationship. As you grow up, at some point the majority of human beings need more than platonic bonding. Usually with, but not limited to, the opposite sex. To have someone to rely upon, and to share more intimate details of our lives. There is no particular age when one can feel that their feelings for another stretch further than the purely platonic, but the word that comes to mind when that happens is *love*! Having such person in your life is a sin. Prohibited and worthy of humiliation, subject to permanent grounding by parents, forced marriage, and even death in many families – known as #honourkillings in the media.

While Bollywood thrives on romantic films, God forbid should you fall in love in real life. Some parents commit suicide in shame if their child's spouse is not of their caste, status or religion. Others cut all connections with them merely because their children choose to marry a partner of their own choosing. Free will to choose your life partner was, I guess, a copy-and-paste error when the Indian constitution was being copied from the British and American one. Oops sorry, I mean 'borrowed'...

The dictionary defines an affair in many ways and one of the meanings is:

1) *An intense amorous relationship, usually of short dur*
   ation.
2) *A sexual relationship between two people who are no*
   t married to each other.

A relationship on the other hand is more like this:

1) *The condition or fact of being related; connection or ass*
   ociation.
2) *Connection by blood or marriage; kinship.*
3) *A particular type of connection existing between people*
   related to or having dealings with each other: has a clos
   e relationship with his siblings.
4) *A romantic or sexual involvement.*

Notice that, while the affair is usually of a short duration, sexually motivated and mostly hidden from the world, a relationship has more potential. A romantic partnership, in particular, usually involves more than mere physical attraction. Alas, third world society – or at least majority of it – fails to discriminate between the two. They don't see that an *affair*, which usually amounts to cheating on a spouse, is different from a person having a healthy romantic *relationship* with another.

This way, adult children are pushed into lying and hiding their love life entirely. Merely to express their love, they often end up in the most dangerous and isolated areas of the city. Last year, my friend was excited to show me the newly developed part of the city called Marine Drive in Lucknow, and one winter evening we went for a long drive. The area is literally walk-worthy, and after a while we parked the car and took a long stroll. As it got darker, I noticed flocks of couples gathering in the dark alleys. The passing cars from the high-speed traffic were only good enough to recognize the silhouettes of one man and another woman – hugging, kissing or simply holding hands and chatting.

My heart is left in pain by the hypocrisy that rules our society. To love, one has to put their life in danger – *this* is the way we treat consensual relationships. When it comes to marriage, it doesn't matter whether a girl consents or not. Normally, she is talked into consenting by luring her with the spouse's money and house. For greedy women who value a materialistic life, that's actually a pretty good deal. They scoop up their father's wealth by demanding a hefty dowry if the guy hasn't already done so, plus they dream of all the gold and cars they'd be able to show off to their neighbourhood and school friends post-wedding.

Oh yeah, speaking of which...

You remember that girl in school? The one you barely ever spoke with, who made you feel that she had no idea you were alive in grade 10? She just sent you a Facebook friend request. Why, you ask? Oh dummy, she's getting married in two months and wants you to like all the pictures, comment on her make-up, and envy how she has landed such a rich husband. The kind that can afford to whisk her away on a European honeymoon, when we all know that her poor parents were forced to give it as part of the dowry deal! Go ahead and accept that freaking request. I dare you!

Chapter 3

The Puberty Blues (and Reds, and Yellows, and Pinks...)

It was the worst day of my childhood. The school toilet was dark, and reeked vigorously of phenyl – a cleaning fluid that would have been used to rinse the waste of the million students that used the toilet previously. Think I'm exaggerating for dramatic effect? This was an Indian school, where each class had about 7 sections with 40 students each. I'm no mathematician, but I'm pretty sure I'm not too far off.

I sat down in the last stall of the large communal washroom, and wondered *what had I done*? Why was God punishing me? Why was this happening to me?

My abdomen hurt like a tractor had gone wild in my uterus, or Nicki Minaj was rehearsing her *Anaconda* dance in my fallopian tubes. Two hours had passed. I could see sunlight scatter on the floor through the high but tiny window. I could see my blurred reflection, and I hated my face. It was time to reflect. I saw the lady janitor drop by few times, but I dared not ask for help. I felt too ashamed, and as a result I hid every time.

My school dress was stained with blood thanks to a new phenomenon in my life; menstruation. There were changes all around and inside of me, and I had not been taught to prepare for these transformations. On the inside, it looked like a crime scene from *Saw 3*.

Although I had an elder sister, we never really talked about this stuff openly. One day when out of the blue (or red, if you prefer a more visceral analogy), I began menstruating and life just crashed around me. I have a blurred memory of what happened and how I dealt with it, but what I remember *perfectly* is the shame attached to the experience.

We were an educated family and pretty modern, but that didn't stretch to open discussions about puberty. In fact I was told not to pray, not to touch certain things, and that since I was now impure, I should wear long and dark clothes. Since I was really a child, I could not handle walking around normally, or sleep in that moon white fragrant linens as you see on advertisements. Tampons still do not exist in India, so the 'go-to' feminine hygiene product a maxi pad the size of Barbie's mattress that could soak up the next Tsunami. It still failed its mission, somehow; and this mission failure would occur mostly during school time when there were these nasty, sticky creatures called 'boys' lurking around.

This was the doomsday scenario for me. I had a stained dress, and I couldn't leave the toilet or ask anybody for help. Apparently, the child that I was felt too ashamed to talk about my problem with anyone. It was about my honour, after all. I rather would have died than shared my indignity. I cried for a while, and fought with God for making me a girl. Then my attention drifted off to the reflection of my face on the floor; the pinkish ugly pimple on my cheek, wondering why it always appeared during this time of the month. That pimple thought was in turn interrupted by some unpleasant, and rather frightening, noises coming from the nearby toilet stall.

Three hours passed, and finally the bell of hope rang. The last class ended and children popped out of the school building like slaves freed from the ship of Spartacus. Finally, I snuck out of the toilet and ran to my class through the empty corridors, still reeking of sweat. I ran away, hung my school bag as low on my back as I could manage, and somehow reached home sitting on a cycle rickshaw.

You see, I was absolutely unaware of what menstruation *was* before it happened with me like some kind of awful accident. I have no idea why, but my mom never discussed it. When I ask now, her straightforward answer is that, *"children must not know about grown up things."* I often find myself wondering why such a grown up thing happens to children, if this is the case.

Recently I was reading Caitlin Moron's *How To Be a Woman*, where she describes her experience. I loved reading about how her sister Caz suggested getting her uterus removed and replaced with an extra pair of lungs, enabling her to smoke when she grew up. Period stories are unique, and range from sad to hilarious.

Menstruation is biological, but periods are social. Menstruation is a perfectly healthy bodily function that is discussed in the Biology class, while periods are those hidden, shameful curses that fall upon us once a month. Menstruation is good; the world needs menstruating girls to create the next generation of humans, so we will have more wars and cars. But periods? Periods are *bad*. An ugly, dirty part of womanhood, that needs to be confined to the four walls of a hygienically questionable school toilet. A menstruating woman can bring a human to life, while a woman on her period is supposed to stay away from praying, the kitchen and even their husband, because she is filthy. In Nepal, menstruating women are sent to exile in huts where sometimes they even die. Google it.

If you need to buy female hygiene products, aka sanitary napkins (tampons are unheard of) in India, the conversation goes something like this.

Girl enters a pharmacy.

Girl looks to the right, looks to left, and slowly passes a small piece of paper to the clerk.

The guy slyly looks at the paper, and gives a secret look back. This is like a James Bond movie!

He then goes at the back of his shop and reaches for a packet of Whisper sanitary pads.

Wraps in newspaper, then another newspaper then a black plastic bag, then a newspaper, then another plastic bag.

Clerk returns, slyly gives the bulky package to girl, your package is ready.

20 rupees please!

Girl leaves, hoping that nobody saw her transaction.

Clerk vigorously washes his hands.

The Wonders of a Tampon

It might be hard to believe for western readers, but I was first introduced to a tampon at the age of 24..

My Portuguese friend Sonia and I reached her home after a long chatty afternoon by the Cardiff Bay. She asked me to make myself comfortable while she placed her bag on the coffee table, and brought a cute looking tin box out. I loved the packaging and asked, "wow, is that a chocolate or candy you are hiding in there?"

She burst out laughing, as I am guessing you might be at this moment. If you don't know what tampons are, you probably are in the third world and don't worry, it's not your fault. I will explain in a few minutes why.

After she finished laughing she explained that it was a tampon. I gave her a blank expression akin to a chimp introduced to quantum mechanics. That was when she realised I really wasn't kidding. Shock came over her that at my age, twelve years after puberty had initially struck, I didn't know what a tampon was. She opened that packaging that had so enraptured me and explained their purpose, giving me two for trial. I had a million questions and my lovely friend calmly explained all about it.

For the uninitiated, a tampon is a cotton wad that is inserted in the vaginal opening that absorbs the blood before it reaches the outer labia. In that way, it helps maintain cleanliness and doesn't restrict movement like a napkin does. You can easily bring the magic of tampons to your world with the aid of Google if you need more information. *Goodbye Barbie mattresses*, I thought to myself.

Never in my life had I waited so excitedly for my monthly cycle like I waited this time. Finally, it began. I did as she had instructed. Filled with fear, I doubted whether I should go through with it or not. But considering the amount of pain I had suffered over the years running around with a mattress stuck between my thighs I had to give it a go. And so I did!

At first, it didn't fit. I was too afraid to push it in, as I was worried. What if it got lost and travelled up in my body? Yes, yes, I know I was 24, but still, I was 12 in tampon years so cut me and my silly worries some slack.

I didn't push it far enough, and it felt very uncomfortable and disgusting. I couldn't take it anymore and needed some motivation.

Now, here comes so some industrial strength 'girl-talk' so don't get queasy. Trigger warning, or whatever you need to know.

I called Sonia and discussed my first time tampon experience. She, being an expert, knew exactly why that was. She assured it wouldn't travel up north in my body; it didn't have a passport so I needn't worry.

I asked how I would know if I had done it correctly, and she told me it would feel like nothing when it is rightly pushed back. She was right; it didn't. Finally, for the first time in my life, I broke free from the clutches of the mattress-shaped sanitary napkin that stifled my movement and often caused leakages at the most unexpected and embarrassing places. Places that included white cushions in a friend's house, or the light pink couches of a classy restaurant. It also happened on a long bus ride to London and a 9-hour long haul flight to New Delhi, but those experiences are too traumatic to recount.

I consider Tampons to be the greatest invention of all time in the female hygiene department. However, India is far from accepting tampon as a regular commercial product. The first time my mom and sister saw a tampon, they weren't as excited as I was. Not only did they fear that my hymen would break and my virginity would be destroyed, erasing my worth in the Indian society as a woman, but also that inserting a tampon could provide me with sexual pleasure. Of course, *that is not what a woman's vagina is for*. It exists only to please our husbands.

I will discuss the myth of virginity at length in the next chapter but for now, if like my mom and sister you don't already know, there is no such thing as 'virginity', and inserting a tampon certainly isn't sexual pleasure. The best part about a tampon is that it feels like nothing. Which I'm sure some women would also claim about their husbands, but that's not for me to say.

When I look back and analyse my menstruation history, I find nothing but shame and disgust. I wish I never had to go through those horrible, embarrassing years of feeling shameful about a very natural and healthy bodily function that took place within me.

Aditi Gupta is a young woman who introduced Menstrupedia to India not too long ago. Not only are women now being told about what menstruation *is*, but Aditi is informing boys about the process and challenging the social stigma of shame. Am I jealous of this generation? Heck yes. Where were these cool, new, exciting period comics and fun wisdom when I was locked inside that stinky toilet for 4 hours waiting for the school day to end?

Other than menstruation, boobs are another cause of society's worry in our culture. It really was a dreadful time of my life was when my breasts began changing. I would look in the bathroom mirror and cry for hours, praying to God that somehow they may disappear. These days, young girls get implants because they want bigger breasts. Personally, I wept for mine to flatten like a tortilla.

Do you know why? Because it was shameful! What I saw around me was that it was shameful to have breasts. I had to always cover them with a scarf or jacket, like I was hiding a loaf of meat stolen from an orphanage. Whenever I would dress, the first thing my mother would notice was whether I was covering my secret appropriately.

My prayers went unanswered. God didn't listen, and my breasts grew. It made me even guiltier when we visited India for holidays and I would notice a street-side jerk staring at me, or other perverts attempting to grope on busy public places like railway stations. I had a body I *hated* being in. I would see other grown women, and my mother who had a grown woman's body, and I saw the shame attached to it.

It's hard to explain in words, but it felt like I was already guilty of *something* by virtue of being a girl. That being a girl was carrying a huge risk on my shoulders; the risk of becoming a shameful disappointment for my family and religion. Boobs and menstruation, the two major biological changes that mark the starting of womanhood, are feared, hidden and despised. It felt that even women – even the people you love most in the world -

would place the 'male-gaze' glasses on when they looked at you, and passed judgment accordingly.

Puberty *does* mark the onset of sexual maturity in a young girl, but it *doesn't* change the person she is. Puberty doesn't make her any less human than anyone else. People fear that with puberty a girl may begin to feel sexual urges or want to explore her sexuality, and this is too much for our families to handle. They prefer to pretend that our sexuality doesn't exist. Our puberty is an illusion, and our sexual urges are locked up inside a big old rotten box, the keys of which are held by our future husbands. Whether we want them to hold those keys or not, they control the operations, the opening and closing of this box, and we are mere contents with no say in the matter whatsoever.

PS. Out of curiosity, I ordered a silicon moon cup from China recently to advance my use of feminine hygiene products. I don't think I'll be giving it a shot anytime soon, simply because I'm not a fan of cleaning up after a crime scene. Tampons are easier to dispose of, so I'm going to continue with them for now.

Chapter 4

·———✦———·

Virginity for Sale – Only $29.95! (FREE worldwide discreet delivery)

O ur society has two kinds of girls. The girls with premium are the ones who are pure. Virgins. Clean like the river Ganges (although the contamination of Ganga is debatable). The other kind deserve to be burnt alive according to the defence lawyers of Nirbhaya's rape case, Mr. Sharma and Mr. Singh.

Sadly enough, the majority of people I have known over the years have beliefs along the lines of this pair of idiotic morons. They may not go as far as to publicly claim to burn the women of their houses (sisters, mothers, friends, cousins) but they *do* disown a woman if she is ever found to have (whisper it quietly) *consented to sexual intercourse*. Women are disowned for being *raped*, so wilful consent to intercourse is way off-brand.

The reason why I wanted to share my observations about this virginity issue is because of the double standards we live in, and the shitty ways that we tell women that their worth is contained in their hymens. This applies to both first *and* third world countries, by the way.

Before I go further into that, however, let me explain the chapter name. Yes, hymens are for sale! At a website called www.hymenshop.com you can buy artificial, fake hymens for $29.95! The funny thing – which made me literally roll on the floor laughing – is that there is even a bulk purchase offer!

You can buy, 2, 3, 4 or 5 together. How stupid do you think men are? Who would believe that their women regained their virginity within 24 hours of penetrative sex? If it's for practice, how many men do you sleep with, to actually practice the hymen breaking, before you make your husband believe he broke your real hymen?

This is the height of the bullshit that surrounds certain cultures and generations.

Why would you want to fool your man into believing you have no sexual history?

Why would you want to marry a man who attaches your worth to a hymen?

How long would a marriage based on the existence of hymen actually last?

Why do we need to create such products that would fool men and provide fake perceptions of women's loyalty?

Why do we put *so much* emphasis on hymens that women are forced to buy fakes to prove their worth?

Why are women attracted to this idea of faking virginity?

What does that tell us about the men of our society?

What does that tell us about the women of our society?

Umm, I guess, it tells us that most men of our generation are judgmental, thoughtless, hypocritical misogynists, while the women of our society are self-obsessed, lying, cheating insecure frauds. Thank God, not all men and women fall into the customer demographics of www.hymenshop.com. But is it really the woman's fault? Would she be purchasing this BS product if men had not defined her sense of self-worth this way?

Why is Virginity a Lie?

Yes, you studied right in your 8th grade Biology class. There is a thing called the hymen located in a girl's vagina, and medical researchers have debated its purpose for years. The hymen is a membrane in the vaginal canal. Doctors are still in disagreement on its function. Many believe that it simply has no particular use to the woman's body, but for sure it has tiny holes in the membrane through which the menstrual blood passes. So, there you go, I just torpedoed the concept of popping that hymen because – guess what? It already has holes in it. And with physical exercise, wear and tear, it gets torn off and sheds gradually.

Yes, there are women within whom the hymen is so tightly intact that it has no holes whatsoever, and these are the women who undergo so much pain that they ultimately visit a doctor to get the hymen removed. If they don't do so, their life may be in danger.

OK, if that was too much for you, here is the best video ever created by College Humor called The Truth About Hymens and Sex. Watch and learn!

https://www.facebook.com/CollegeHumor/videos/1015337374
7252807/?fref=nf

Regardless of what popular culture thinks, can we puhhlleaaseeeee come out of our caves and see people for their personalities and talents, rather than judging their worth based on their hymens?

And while I am at it, let me tell you another thing. Because in Asian and Middle Eastern cultures, there is so much pressure on young girls to remain virgins until they marry, they find other ways to engage in sexual activity.

You know what I mean right?

The kinkier ones... The fifth base level ones... The uh... the um...

Oh screw it, let me say it – oral and anal sex, damn it.

Wow. Imagine a conservative guy who is so persistent that he asks before the wedding if the girl is virgin or not, ends up marrying a girl who has been to fifth base!

Huh, she's certainly going to teach him a lot in bed. Enjoy your virgin, you asshole of a man.

Chapter 5

The Wedding Trap

The Grooming Technique

Pardon me for being blunt here, but at times the subtle messages I hear all around me signal towards a very specific place for women in society. Remember that sex robot thing Howard from *The Big Bang Theory* was building? Yes, women's existence is summed up into that; a tool to assist the lives of men. We are walking and talking set of body parts that can be used by men and children at different times.

Now you must be thinking, "oh come on Shahla! Isn't that an exaggeration?"

No, it isn't. It may not be true for me, because I grew up in the shadow of a feminist father and my life has been different. The only reason you are reading this book is because of the lifestyle and freedom he gave me. Sadly, that isn't the case for most girls. The ones who have a comfortable life with their parents are not permitted to remain in that comfort zone for long. The day they are married, they turn into the robot I was talking about.

I couldn't say this out loud until I read this research by the OECD.   Guess what? India ranked the worst. Yup, surprise surprise!

A recent survey by the Organization for Economic Co-operation and Development (OECD) says that an average Indian man has the dubious distinction of spending all of 19 minutes a day on routine housework, among the lowest total in the world. Indian *women*, meanwhile, spent a huge 298 minutes on routine housework such as cooking, laundry, pets, home maintenance etc. Even in the most equal societies of the western world, there is no country with a 50/50 share. Women do the majority of the household chores.

This may seem trivial to some of you, but this work has an unaccounted economic value. If someone would hire a maid to do all this work around the house, it would cost them a considerable sum of money. Women don't even get appreciation in most homes for their dedication.

So, the condition in most households is crappy as you can imagine. Why do women get married then? Why are they so excited and crazy about the idea of a wedding?

Instead of that question, let's ask how society brainwashes girls into getting married? I say *girls*, not women, because in third world, most females are married while they are still girls.

That's a technique used by pimps and human traffickers called 'grooming' that I came across in a course that I took. Grooming is defined as, "when someone builds an emotional connection with a child to gain their trust for the purposes of sexual abuse or exploitation." Or in this case, marriage.

Grooming starts early, as parents start talking to their babies about how pretty they would look when they are dressed up as a bride almost from the cradle. The baby usually either gives an ape-like blank expression, farts or chuckles, depending on how full their little belly is. But it begins.

I could not believe when my sister was talking to me about her first delivery experience, and the story of my niece's birth. Just like those theatrical Bollywood mothers, her eyes filled with tears and she announced, "I can already feel the pain I'll experience when I send her away to her husband."

You can probably guess at my reaction?

"Are you nuts? What is this, 1923? Nobody is sending anybody away."

Then she pouted and said, "I am going to find her a house husband so he can come and live with us so my daughter wouldn't have to be sent away."

As the feminist, buzz-killing, mood-breaker that I am, I rolled my eyes and replied, "why don't you let her grow up and choose who she wants to be with, instead of trying to arrange a child marriage? And whether she even wants to marry, and when, if at all..."

My sister said nothing but gave me her fabled 'stop-with-your-liberated-woman-crap-its-still-1760-in-India' look.

So it's strange, but we train little girls to think of their wedding as the greatest day of their lives. While my sister often says these shiny-tempting wedding things to my niece, I teach her kickboxing from YouTube videos in secret. By the way, I am also her hair idol, her dressing idol, and dance idol. I can't believe she has shown half the city my crazy dance on an Arabic song that my sister recorded secretly. I did my hair ombre blond on one occasion that I went home. After I left, anywhere she would find a golden thread, she would bring it to her mom and yell "dekho! Shalu khala ka baal" which means, "look! Aunt Shalu's hair."

Now, imagine this intelligent young girl having to spend the rest of her life washing dishes and feeding others. I am not saying that's wrong, but is this the best she could do? Is this the best that we could *all* do, as women? Is that all we were born for? Is there nothing else to our life?

There are women who believe and proclaim that the best day of their lives or the most important day of their life is their wedding day. If you think the same, I would invite you to think about this – there are a number of days in our lives that are certainly more important, including:

The first day you went to school, with your parents standing at the gate, looking at you with love-filled fearful eyes, hoping the teacher handles you with love and care inside.

The first day you learn about puberty, or the day you experience it, depending upon what you were told in advance and how your experience was.

The first time you have a dream and announce, "when I grow up I want to be a –"

The first time you fall in love, have your heart broken, and learn that you deserve better.

The day you leave school and enter college or university to achieve a life you always knew was possible.

When you travel solo to a new country first time in your life.

The first time you see *Bridget Jones' Diary* or *Sex and the City* (don't judge me, come on, those are filled with golden nuggets of wisdom such as when Samantha compares marriage with Botox. Remember? No? OK, you can pretend. That's fine.)

All of us may have many different memorable days, when we achieved something or lost something, but a wedding is neither. If you think of marriage like an achievement, and that by getting married you achieved something, I'm sorry to say that your standards are very low. Getting married is not an achievement. Keeping a marriage strong and alive is. Read that again.

Change in relationship status isn't a big deal. It is not that by getting married you achieved a person as a prize for doing something great. Either way, a spouse isn't a prize that would remain the same all through your life. Especially before and just after wedding, you never know what the person would turn out to be like. Especially in Indian culture, where others arrange 90% or more of weddings. How would you know what you 'achieved' is worth it? But in our culture, if you want to dream, dream of a wedding.

Likewise, if you want to think, think of a man.

If you want to hope, hope that you get married ASAP.

If you want love, get impregnated on the very first wedding night like a desperate creepy cave woman who has no idea what birth control looks like, and celebrate your first wedding anniversary with a screaming baby in your arm who is pulling your hair in that special picture where you are trying to hide your frustration with a fake smile and pinching your husband under the table asking him to hold the baby while you fix your hair.

Huh. That was a long one.

So, this way, our girls are groomed to build all of their dreams, hopes and aspirations around one freaking awful day – their wedding day. Screw the seventy years that follow, starting tomorrow – wedding day! And God bless you if that happens to fall in summer and you live in the plains of India. In the USA and UK we idolize the June wedding...the summer plaza wedding...

A June wedding in India is a wedding in hell.

You may imagine love in the air, but it's not. That's just 100% moisture that makes it impossible to put even the best of foundation on your skin. Yes, Dior, you fail back there.

If you think about the appropriate clothing for such weather you may have options, but sadly you cannot wear a bikini to an Indian wedding. Doing so may result in a stroke for the elderly attendees, and unwanted erections in young adolescent boys and perverts. The latter covers the majority of men in attendance, including the caterer, the DJ, the groomsmen and often the groom himself.

So, if you're lucky enough your wedding day does not fall in summer as is arranged by the decision makers (parents of both parties, the relatives, the cousin from USA, the aunt who lives in Australia, the religious community leaders, the respected elderly of the neighbourhood, and the groom – basically, everybody but the bride, for whom this is supposedly the most important day of her life), you may have temporary relief.

When young girls are groomed, their heads are filled with talk of shiny things, expensive jewellery, fancy designer clothes, lots of gold, large buffets of various cuisines, and attendance of your relatives, friends, neighbours, community members, relatives of the relatives, and often their other relatives too. The more people who attend your wedding, the more people are shown your dress and your father's wealth. It is also the time for the family to collect gifts and cash from the people they have been giving gifts and cash to at their weddings and events – think of it as the world's most reliable short-term loan system.

To make the dress, make-up and jewellery stuff attractive to us, we are not allowed to dress fancy or wear make-up as single girls. This varies from house to house, but in most conservative Muslim households, young girls wear the least vibrant colours (think beige – the colour of band aids and almonds), and absolutely no make-up or jewellery. They say that this way, when you do put on make-up on your special day, you will be a sight to behold!

You know what? I agree. Because you have never used make-up, you don't know that the beautician hired to doll you up is using cheap foundation that will look cakey in your wedding pictures, and the shape of your eyes is fighting a losing battle against the eye shadow colours. Finally you end up looking like a monkey in the circus and an absolute showstopper! And by the way, many weddings I have been to do not go through the pains of hiring a professional beautician, leaving the bride at the mercy of a loudly made up cousin or second cousin that looks sexy and leaves their husband drooling. Or a single, modern, educated woman living abroad.

Just as an aside, I have dolled up five brides in my lifetime.

Through saving myself from marriage and learning from looking very closely at five marriages and five divorces, I found out the things what they won't tell you before you tie the knot:

- This day, you will not only become the wife but also the mother of an overgrown man-child, who you have to feed, clean and do his laundry (not always, granted, but most of the time)

- Like you charge your phone, most husbands need a charging at least once every six hours – a boost to the male ego. Hours vary with size, model and generation.

- Your life is not just between you and your spouse, but you will find everybody else's nose in your business.

- There is a high chance there will be no honeymoon, or a honeymoon with the entire family from the groom's side. Very few lucky brides get chance to spend time with their husbands, and those that do mostly hail from high-income modern families.

- When you have an argument with your husband, there *will* be other people's nose in it.

- 2, 3 or 4 years into the marriage, your husband will grow completely bored of you and prefer to spend quality time with *Candy Crush*.

- If you don't work for yourself, you may face financial difficulties depending on the income and educational background of your in-laws. I have seen the wives of doctors and engineers ask their parents for money and groceries in secret, because their husbands will neither let them work nor give them any money for housekeeping.

- If you *do* work, your in-laws will expect you to give them your hard-earned money.

- You may have seen Indian daily soaps on TV, where daughters-in-law are all dressed up and jewelled up all the time. This is a lie. Doing as many household chores as a typical Indian wife does, you're more to likely to end up looking like a cat in a washing machine.

- The larger the family, the more work you do.

- There will be immense pressure from all sides to fall pregnant immediately. Whether you know each other well enough or not, whether you earn sufficient income or not, and whether you both *want* a baby at all or not is absolutely inconsiderable.

When you give birth, Indian hospitals don't allow the romantic husband sitting by the wife holding her hand wiping her brow tradition. This is India we are talking about. There are billions of us. It's more like a poultry farm or factory; chickens lying on a roller, workers doing what needs to be done and passing on to the other without thought and emotion. OK, maybe not *that* mechanical, but it is quite cold and heartless. I visited few hospitals where you can see pregnant women getting sonograms in open hallways, and rooms filled with women yelling like a train station. There's no time for emotion, selfies and balloons and all the stuff that you see in Hollywood movies, or actual hospitals in the first world.

Hence, the trap I was talking about is clearly visible when you lay in a public hospital bed because your in-laws were too stingy to get you a private room with AC, your body is prodded and poked with needles and glucose, and your in-laws are waiting desperately for you to stand up and run home to clean their clothes and cook as usual. And, *of course*, your cold and distant husband acts like he has no clue what the hell has happened, and that he had nothing to do with it. He isn't interested in changing the baby's diaper, and he's probably pissed off with you for giving birth to a baby girl instead of a son and heir.

That's when you realise that the one-day celebration, the make-up boxes, the clothes, the jewellery, *was not worth it.*

Then you feel jealous of your ugly cousin, who is tagged as the unweddable spinster by your community.

The Arranging of Marriage

So now that you have read about the stark facts and probable situations that you might face after your one-day wedding celebration, you may want to take things slow.

An interesting time is when your family is desperately looking for your would-be spouse, and you start to live somewhat like an army soldier. Anytime there can be a trumpet blown that so-and-so family is coming to visit and you have to know how to be ready at the battlefield – in this case, your living room – within minutes.

A friend of mine has had immense practice of this, and she shares her experience with a heavy heart. She says there is a very particular ensemble of dress, shoes and scarf to be donned when she is the showpiece for a prospective groom's family. There is a special section for snacks laid out, and nobody is allowed to eat them except the applicant groom and his family. Sadly, the snacks counter had been re-filled many times but the groom is yet to be found.

Amusing sideswipes aside, the heart of my friend weeps when her own family treats her like a piece of furniture to be sold to the highest bidder. This totally dehumanises us as women, and sadly the older generations just don't seem to understand this. For them, this is how a marriage is *supposed* to take place.

On the other hand, there is a guy I know who keeps rejecting girls. His family will show him a picture, talk of his balding hairline or lonely life, and force him to visit a girl's home. When he runs out of excuses, he will go along, smiling and nodding, and later claim that he isn't interested. His family is known in the community as the 'snack-gobbling groom family', because all they do is visit strange houses, fill up on the food and never call back. His brother once told me that there are streets in the city where he cannot pass by without putting on big goggles and hat so no one recognizes him. I don't know what's his deal – some people say he is gay, others that he is asexual, but *do* know his family are known as the snack killers.

I was once quite close to getting engaged, but thank God I was saved. The guys' mother and I had nothing in common except for our lady parts, and hers were obviously considerably more wrinkled and saggy. Whenever she would have to strike up a conversation with me, either in person or on phone, she would ask me about food. What did I cook? Did I know *how* to cook? It seemed less like a conversation between a potential mother- and daughter-in-law, and more like Gordon Ramsey going nuts on me for screwing up a caviar appetiser on *Kitchen Nightmares*. She never actually *told* me to fuck off with her tongue, but the message was there in her eyes.

I knew the guy well and had high hopes, but I didn't know his family at all. When we were introduced, it didn't go farther than the cooking discussion. The guy was perfectly nice until his family was involved. *Then* he wanted me to pretend to be more like the ideal bahu – the smiling, nodding woman whose tongue had been snipped, and has mere cotton balls in her skull.

Me writing this book would tell you, I have more brain cells than cotton balls in my skull. As you may expect, I dumped his sorry ass.

Chapter 6

———— ✦ ————

The Vomit of Love

This chapter is about love as-they-know-it-and-make-you-believe-in-it.

It was a usual summer evening in New Delhi, and Nina had just climbed out of the shower. She was super excited, as she hadn't had to cook dinner on this particular this evening. Her husband, a software engineer (it's not just a cliché, people) Sameer was on his way home and promised to bring her favourite Mughlai food, kebabs and bread. Sameer had been out of work for months and they had been surviving on bitter gourds and brinjals. Just last week he received his first salary from the new company he had joined, and things were getting back on track.

Excited as Nina was, she lost track of time dressing and getting dolled up for some after dinner delight, if you know what I mean and I'm sure that you do (and if you don't, go back and re-read Chapter 3). Sameer got home earlier than usual and waited outside the bathroom for a few minutes before she realised and stepped out, apologising.

It was all so romantic. She lit candles as the Delhi skyline darkened with the onset of night, then brightened thanks to the moon of a bright summer evening. Nina ran back and forth and arranged the plates and the dinner Sameer brought on the little dining table as they watched the latest episode of *Sasural Simar Ka* on TV (check this out for yourself if you must, but watch at your own risk.)

It was special. She had not seen Sameer in such a good mood for so long. Tonight, he served her food with his own hands. As she would take a bite, he gazed deeply into her eyes and smiled (hold on to that smile).

She loved the delicious kebabs and, to her surprise, Sameer also brought her favourite drink to go with the dinner. Since she got married to Sameer, her husband alone had decided what she put in her mouth. Coca Cola was resolutely *not* on the approved list. Not because it's unhealthy or anything – it was absolutely OK when Sameer didn't have to buy it and they went to a dinner party. Coca Cola was banned because it was one of the things Nina liked, and she wasn't *allowed* to like things.

So, as you can imagine, this was a special night because her husband brought her a bottle of Cola! I mean, how lucky is a woman whose husband brings her a bottle of fizzy pop after just 18 months of marriage, right?

All through dinner, Nina was busy sharing her feelings and thanking him for everything while Sameer spent 99% of the time just watching her eat and staring into her eyes, smiling.

"Why did you stop?" Sameer asked when her plate was empty.

'Oh, I'm done, I've eaten more than my usual meal today," she smiled and nodded.

"No, you barely ate anything. You said you loved kebabs from Karims. I got them for you, and you say you are finished after just two? Come on, please eat just one more. I got them for you with so much love. Have just one more, for my sake," he insisted.

"Alright, but just one – and only because you care so much about me," Nina replied as she slid one more round patty of the spicy beef kebab on her plate. As she munched and savoured every bite, she shared the news of her day. How the lady next door kept bothering her for sugar, and her plans to buy curtains for their naked apartment window.

She took a final bite and she stood up saying, "hold on, let me bring dessert. You'll love what I made." As she excitedly began to pace towards the kitchen, she heard some words... words that she thought could not be real.

"Who are you to decide what I will love, bitch?"

She turned around and asked, "did you said something?"

"I said who the fuck are *you* to decide what *I* will love or not?" Sameer replied, making it increasingly clear this time.

"I'm sorry. I didn't mean to..."

"Sorry for what? What *did* you mean, huh?"

'Sameer, did I say something wrong? Why are you getting mad at me?'

"Oh, *I* am the one getting mad! You're the innocent child here, who doesn't know what time to get out of the bathroom so her tired husband can come home from work and take a shower?" yelled Sameer, grabbing Nina's hair and pulled her to the living room.

"Sameer, I'm really sorry. I was so *happy* this evening, I just didn't realise, and it was just five minutes..."

"Just five minutes?"

Instantly came the first tight slap on her sad face.

"How dare you trivialise my needs over yours? I'm the one working all day, making money trying to run this house, while you sleep in that fucking bed your idiot father gave you. And you're trying to tell me that I don't deserve to use the bathroom when I'm home?"

Another slap, this time on the left cheek.

"Sameer, I'm sorry. I promise this won't happen ever again, I swear, I'm begging you, please don't hurt me. Please..." she pleaded as he dragged her to the floor, continuing to slap furiously.

"You're damn right you won't do it again, I will make you remember the consequences of forgetting about your husband's arrival."

"Sameer, what happened to you? Just a minute ago you were so nice to me, feeding me my favourite food, and now within seconds you are someone else?"

Sameer laughed. "So you think I was feeding you that food for my pleasure? No darling, *that's* not what gave me pleasure.

My pleasure will be to see it back up," and he began punching Nina in the belly.

She cried, and begged, and apologised, but Sameer's plan to see her throw up everything she had eaten in her life was powerful. He punched her stomach until nothing but water and blood was left to regurgitate.

Today, two years after that damned night, Nina lives with her parents and has started her own company following my business advice. Her husband is being treated for psychological problems. She divorced Sameer ultimately, but it took many more such wretched dinners until she realised the marriage was unsustainable.

When Nina tells me the story, she is still convinced that her loving husband is not the man who beat her up. She says, with tears in her eyes, that like a million other times – even that night – a few hours after she vomited the food he had fed her with love, he came to her and said, "I love you so much, I can't handle hurt from you."

He took her to the bed and had sex. I can't call it lovemaking. If you want me to be specific, it's marital rape as her consent was negative. *You* try to have marital relations with a man who just punched the life out of you for spending five extra minutes in the bathroom. I dare you.

I pity her when she asks me with a perplexed face, "how can he love me and strangle me to death at the same time?"

Love is the easiest way to fool a woman. But do we really *know* what love is?

I'm not going into Shakespearean descriptions of what love is, and I may not know exactly what it is. But I know for sure is that what it's *not*. Love is not selfish, hurtful, egotistical and controlling. Those things, by default, cancel love. It's like oil and water. They can't mix.

Men throw around the word love thoughtlessly, to excuse their bad behaviour. It's not love when a man tries to control your life, and he says he can't live without you while he is strangling your throat. That's not love, it's *obsession*. It's a psychological state where controlling another person's life and showing power over their trivial decisions gives a man the feeling of being powerful and masculine.

I don't care how many arguments you give me saying, "it's love, but..."

Sorry, but I call bullshit on that definition of love.

Love is not a blurred, grey area. If it hurts, it isn't love. Period. End of the line.

I'm not saying you cannot have an argument with people you love. Of *course* you can. But when you love somebody, you never stoop to seeking revenge for silly things. You don't throw their past in their face, insult their families or humiliate their existence. Love doesn't contain abuse.

Losers try to wrap the word abuse in the cosy, heart-shaped blanket of love. It's easy to confuse a woman with that word. But guess what, sweetheart; it's also the oldest trick in the book. And it's only a matter of time until a woman realises this, and decides that she has to vomit this so-called-love out of her life.

Chapter 7

The Man with the Intrusive Penis

A*piss in public will bring you relief.*
A kiss in public will get you killed.

Sounds like a weird culture, doesn't it? Welcome to India in 2017.

My sister and her neighbour friend were on their way home from college on a fine afternoon almost ten years ago. Their bus would drop them at a stop a hundred feet from their home, and they would walk past by this street each and every day.

In full, broad daylight, they noticed a man rush before them and began urinating, his body facing the wall and his head facing them sideways. As is an Indian woman's first and natural instinct, they got their heads down and ignored the incident, feeling awkward (for his part, the man in question seemed to feel no such shame). They reached home uneasy and disturbed by the incident, but hey, that is the India we live in. People (apologies, let me rephrase – *men*) have the right to pee in public, and you cannot point fingers at them. Doing so will make *you* the villain of the piece.

The next day they spent their time in dental college, fixing teeth and dreaming of futures as professional dentists. After a long day of hard work and daydreaming, a familiar awkward sight on their way home once again confronted them; the same penis-waving man, once again rushing in front of them. Standing at the same wall and repeating the same activity, and presumably it was no prettier second time around. Horrified and harassed, they thanked God that they were not alone on either occasion and hurried home once again. Being alone could have easily resulted in rape or another serious sexual assault, as the road in question was lined with empty buildings on either side, and a hot summer afternoon tended to be particularly quiet in the area.

Now, for a woman it becomes a tough call to decide whether you *are* being sexually harassed on the street, or simply being a bitch by pointing out and questioning a poor innocent man's right to pee in public. You don't *want* to be either, but sadly one of them has to be true, right?

Noticing the same unwanted view of his intrusive penis for five consecutive days, the girls decided to finally speak up. Alas, this wasn't easy. Talking to your father about a man's disturbing penis can be painfully awkward, especially in an Indian household (though I'm assured by Western friends that it's not ideal dinner conversation with their parents in other cultures either). Nevertheless, they narrated the gross incident involving the unimpressive penis and the disgusting shit of a man attached to it.

My father owns a gym, and as a result has a minimum of ten pumped up Arnold Schwarzenegger-wannabes perpetually on tap, just a phone call away. He called one of them, who was the then-instructor, and asked him to 'take care of the matter'.

The matter indeed was taken care of. The next day, when their bus dropped the girls, the instructor hid behind a nearby tree and watched the events unfold in the same regrettable way. As was now standard, the pervert came along with his desperate penis and began showing off his soon-to-be-endangered assets to the girls.

Our macho second-hand Arnold pounced on him from behind the tree, and thus began *Die Hard 6 – The Pervert Edition*. The girls ran home, and we later heard that a gang of guys had cracked the exhibitionist's bones in addition to seemingly offering a handful of useful tips on how to avoid strolling around in public with your penis out.

Years later, I still walk past the same streets near my home and not much has changed. Unlike my sister, I never happened to be an unwilling spectator of a one-man show, but I have heard things. We are constantly reminded that we are girls, and we must not go out of the house unless accompanied and chaperoned. On my vacation this year, my parents were so worried that they didn't allow me to go out after sunset alone. Not even once.

This loving imprisonment was not borne of oppression, but rather fear of what they see in the news. It's not as though they would lock me up if I stepped outside – they sent me to the UK for my studies for crying out loud! However, they have zero faith that I may return safe from the street outside our door. If I do defy them and go against their will, they would remain worried until I came back. Hence, I didn't go out alone after dark. It just seemed better for all concerned.

One may wish that the story could have been different. If the girls knew self-defence, they may have felt safer or been in a better position to handle the guy themselves.

And that is where we go wrong. Why should girls take even 1% responsibility for being harassed on the street? Why should girls be locked behind walls and not go out at any freaking time of the day or night?

Probably, because it is easier for people to lock up their girls rather than take a long, hard look at the crime in the street and put in the hard work required to combat it. As a basic human habit, they choose the easy way. They lock up the girls. This results in a severe and dangerous mindset that women who stay at home like a slave are modest and pure, while those who go out for work, shopping, walks or any other damn reason are somehow sluts and deserve any unpleasantness that comes their way.

In the above incident, one may question my choices when it comes to taking matters in our hands and responding with violence. I am a non-violent person, and do not believe in mob mentality. In fact I have deliberately spoken and written against mob mentality and violence over all my body of work. And yet, I didn't even flinch when my gym coach and his cohorts enacted some physical retribution upon this pervert.

Maybe because I know that we had the privilege of *using* that power in that moment, and using that privilege to stop a pervert from harassing girls seemed like a wise decision that bore instant results. The ends justified the means, if you will.

On the other hand, we could have complained to the police. That's what they are paid for, after all. Sadly, the sight of a man peeing on the street is so unremarkable as to be almost *expected* as far as Indian law enforcement are concerned. They would deem such a complaint as trivial, allowing the pervert to go free and reoffend with just a few abusive words in his ear for his troubles.

There is no sex offender record in India, and in the Indian courts there are pending cases that would take 7,000 years to solve at the current rate. The game plan of the government is to wait until people die, so they can scrap a few of those pending cases. In a nation that thinks this way, depending upon the judiciary for punishing a pervert for public urination and harassment while he is at it seems a bit redundant.

Hence we went with the *Die Hard 6 – The Pervert Edition* strategy. And I'll say again – rightly or wrongly, I am not sorry about that. And if you think that I should be, maybe ask yourself if you are partaking in victim blaming without even realising it. Does this man's right to wave his reproductive organs at disinterested young women overrule their right to walk home from college without being exposed to such a sight?

I have tackled harassment in my own way in life. Once, at the age of 13, I remember we were in Saudi Arabia. The family were out shopping and for some reason my father parked in front of a row of shops and popped inside. I was in the front seat, and my mother and sister were in the back. As you can probably imagine, we were already covered in the Muslim Burqa from top to bottom, with only our eyes visible.

One jerk, sitting right in front of the car, began staring. His unwelcome glances were despicable, and with the passing time began to feel increasingly alarming. I casually took off my shoes and began pointing at him. I waved my wrist gently from left to right, and right to left, as a mirror that showed his reflection was the same as the dirt of my shoe.

Had it been India and had it been ten years later, I would have created a scene; I did so once at an airport. On my last trip to India, I had unfortunately taken the flight to Delhi that lands at 2am. Since there is no domestic flight to my hometown before 6am, I had to spend the wee small hours of the night in the airport lounge. Not the most picturesque of surroundings, but before you ask – no, I could not have stepped out of the airport. This is *Delhi* – the rape capital of India. Searching for a hotel alone at 2am would have been a decision that no intelligent woman would make. Conversely, I have been called paranoid by other women for being adverse about venturing outside Delhi airport, to which I say once bitten, twice shy. You know how once bitten by a dog, a person is always wary around dogs? Now think of that in human terms, as the specimens I'm referring to have none of the lovable nature of faithful canines.

As I waited in the almost empty lounge, a young man walked past and sat right in front of me. I had my iPod on and pretended to be in some other world with Taylor Swift and Lady Gaga. Within a few minutes, I noticed his blunt and lame staring eyes. Still pretending not to notice, I casually took my bag and went to the flight boarding announcement screen, thereby moving to another spot.

You may not be surprised, but within five minutes he too had moved and sat straight across from me. I changed my position again, and so did he. Thankfully my boarding time was announced and I left the lounge. Guess what? So did he! And now he began following me. He would walk past by me and then wait for me to catch up, then he would slow down until I jumped on another flat elevator and then he would pass by. I had never seen anything so lame in my life; what kind of a sick game of cat and mouse was he playing? I avoided confrontation because it was early, I was tired after a 9-hour long haul flight, and I didn't even want to look at his stupid face. Alas, his actions left me no choice.

Eventually I stopped right next to him and asked, "what the hell is your problem, jerk?" Shocked by my reaction he blurted out a non-committal "what? who? huh?" Folding my sleeves, I said, "do you want me to call airport security right now?"

Cue the puppy face and attempts to play dumb (not much of a challenge, I'd wager). "I don't know what you are talking about, madam."

Me, boiling in anger, responded with, "listen joker, don't act innocent with me. You are lucky there are no airport police here right now, but if you follow me for one more second, you will be jailed. So back off". Turning my head, words like, "bastard, moron, idiot..." and more came tumbling out of my mouth like monsoon rain.

It worked! He stopped following me and I reached home safely. There are women who think that it is a matter of pride for beautiful girls to be catcalled and harassed. They attract men because of their feminine charms, and that harassment is proof of their beauty over other women. If you are one of those women, trust me, there is nothing to feel proud of about being catcalled. The same woman whose body parts they find so admirable soon becomes a bitch or slut within 15 seconds of rejection.

Street harassment in India is part of our daily life, mind you. The most *aggressive* kind. As the world progresses in technology and science, Indian life has progressed more in more terms of violence against women. Earlier men could harass women outside on the street like the guy from the story. Now, they can do so on our phones and our homes through cyber crime. Most people recommend that – with the growing crimes against women on the street, women stay home if they want to be safe. As cyber harassment began to increase, then came an announcement that women must abandon Facebook, stay away from Twitter, and they dare not be on Whatsapp.

Does avoiding any kind of communication with the outside world solve the problem of violence against women?

No.

I suggest we dig our own graves inside our homes, and lay there quietly as we wait for our deaths. If there were no more women, there couldn't possibly be violence against women, right? Problem solved.

But hey, wait! Who will then cook, and clean, and be used as a punching bag for the holy men of our society?

PS. Women in graves aren't safe from rape either. Necrophilia is trending in India. A recent news incident surfaced where a young woman in her twenties died during childbirth. Two days after the funeral, her body was found outside the grave and a gang of rapists were caught.

Considering how far perverts can go with their shitty desperations, beating up the man with the intrusive penis doesn't sound so bad to me. Sue me!

Paranoid Women

From my bra strap to my period blood

Everything has become political.

You call me crazy because I'm scared to walk alone at night.

You call me paranoid when I don't step out of the airport on my own.

You laugh at the pepper spray in my purse and you say I'm overreacting when I get uncomfortable with talk of sexual assault.

Once bitten by a dog, you'll always be wary around dogs.

How about being bitten by two dogs?

Does that alertness still look crazy?

How about bitten by three dogs? All that you knew and trusted?

Would you call it paranoia?

Yes, rape victims are cautious.

Yes, they know that not every man in the world is a rapist.

But since any man *can* be a rapist, it's only a matter of which one.

Call me paranoid all you want.

I don't expect you to understand.

Only those bitten know what it's like.

To have lived through that chilling bite.

The bite of a man you trusted

Ripping apart your flesh from your bones

While your eyes freeze in shock and beg to let go

He just doesn't get that no means no.

Chapter 8

The Irony of Sleeping with a Stranger

I saw a meme on the Internet few days ago that said, "Indian girls are traditional and dignified. They don't add strangers on Facebook; they marry them".

My reaction? "Sounds about right."

The sleep on wedding night rule

My neighbourhood is called The Girl's Club, because most families have female children. Growing up in this community was both weird and fun. Weird, because I was a total outcast despite being a girl. How, you ask?

Well, for starters, I was one of the few who went to a co-ed school. Then occasionally, my classmates showed up at my door to exchange notes or books, and obviously on festivals and birthdays. I was instantly seen as the 'modern' one. I didn't care, but as you can probably imagine, my mother did.

One fine autumn evening, a few of us girls were hanging out on my neighbour's balcony, chatting about marriages. I was 18 and the rest of them were in the same age range. One of the typical ones announced with a cheeky twinkle in her eye, "did you know it is mandatory to have sex on your wedding night, otherwise the food served in the reception ceremony is cursed by God?"

Others gasped and made shy faces and discussed cheerfully how they were not into it because of the guy being a stranger and all (shocking how positive they felt about the guy being a *stranger*), but they would certainly through with it for the sake of being a good religious wife.

Others chuckled and mentioned how their elder cousins or friends got married and how awkward their wedding nights have been. Bear in mind that this was in 2002, before smartphones were prevalent in India, and thus porn was hard to access in public internet cafes – even more so for girls. These nuptials were awkward because:

- The groom was a total stranger.
- All their life they had been taught to see sex as evil and sinful.
- They had absolutely no idea what the heck to do, apart from feel disgusted with themselves or ripping the husband's clothes to shreds.
- Most of the time, it didn't turn out to be the beautiful, surprising night they were taught to expect.

I didn't make any comment there, but it certainly disturbed me. First of all, I never for once thought that I would marry a total stranger. Secondly, Islam doesn't have such nonsense rules as far as I knew. Thirdly, if the consent is not voluntary and enthusiastic, it clearly isn't sex in the marital bed – it's *rape*.

As I suspected, it was a made-up thing. There was no such evidence of this custom being Islamic as far as my research indicated. Now, you can clearly imagine who may have invented this stupid legend based on who gains most from it.

Women are on both extreme ends of this particular spectrum. Either they are totally desperate and would go to any lengths to satisfy their curiosity around sex, or they are queens of chastity who hate any form of sexual contact, even years after marriage. Psychologically, it has been ingrained in the minds of some women that sexual gratification is a bad thing.

The sad part is that those who actually *enjoy* sex are happy to hide behind the stupid custom excuse, because if they openly talk about such matters they would be slut shamed and looked down upon by their husbands. So, no matter how much they *want* and enjoy sex, they are forced to act like prudes – just so the precious flower of a husband will not think of them as easy.

Or worse, and whisper this one quietly, *a woman with a sexually active past.*

The sickening thing behind all this is that these women act in such a manner to make their husband chase them for sex, or worse, *force* them. Somehow, this is empowering for the man. This concept of forcing your wife for sex was very visible all through Bollywood movies until the late 90s, and while women on TV are more openly embracing their sexuality, in real life the dynamics are still that from the 80s.

Gentle play between a husband and wife? Some teasing and a little attitude? These things can spice up a relationship. But what happens when there is a clear no?

According to the United Nations Population Fund, The International Center for Research on Women surveyed more than 9,200 men across seven Indian states. One-third of them admitted to having forced a sexual act on their wives, while 60 per cent said they'd used some form of violence to assert dominance over their partners. If these statistics do not frighten and outrage you, you may be reading the wrong book.

Another 2014 report, by researcher Aashish Gupta of the Rice Institute, found that women are 40 times more likely to be sexually assaulted by their husband than a stranger. Gupta concluded that fewer than 1 per cent of sexual assaults within marriage are reported to police.

For most people, a woman's irrevocable consent comes by default when she marries a man. She becomes her husband's property, and she has no rights over her own body after marriage – the moment she signs that marriage certificate, she also signs away *herself*, body and soul. Indian Law doesn't recognize marital rape as a punishable offence. In fact, it very clearly states that every act of forced sex is punishable by law *except* in the case of a husband forcing his wife.

When this issue was raised by activists in 2015, the Indian Minister of State for Home, Haribhai Parathibhai Chaudhary, said that the concept of marital rape does not apply in the Indian context because our culture and values are different from the rest of the world. His exact verbiage was:

"It is considered that the concept of marital rape, as understood internationally, cannot be suitably applied in the Indian context due to various factors, including level of education, illiteracy, poverty, myriad social customs and values, religious beliefs, mindset of the society to treat marriage as a sacrament,"

First of all, I don't think marital rape internationally means something else to India. Marital rape is sex without consent with of your wife in *every* country. And every planet too, if aliens are listening. And if you are, I'd welcome to welcome our new intergalactic overlords. Try not to be jerks, we have enough of those on Earth already thanks.

Secondly, if marriage is a sacrament, then isn't rape *contaminating* the holy sacrament? Why should such an act be protected from becoming a criminal offense?

Thirdly, different levels of education, literacy, poverty, customs and beliefs have not stopped men from forcing their wives in even one of those levels. Doesn't that mean that literacy, education yada yada yada, is all just irrelevant to marital rape?

Returning to the topic of marrying strangers, a few days ago my sister sent me a photograph of a young man and his matrimonial catalogue; i.e, bio data. At first I almost had a panic attack because I thought it was for me. I thought to myself "oh no, not this again..."

Then I opened the Whatsapp window and discovered that her best friend's younger sister is getting married, and she sent the bio data and photograph to all her friends to get their opinion. I don't know if I should bang my head on the wall over people's stupidity, or curse myself for bothering to progress while my people remain vain and happy in their caves.

As for these two friends, my sister is a dentist and her friend, the woman parading a strange man's bio data, is an engineer. Both housewives by the way, because professional work is for educated men while educated women are to sit at home and wash his knickers.

So anyway, when I saw that I simply responded, "tell your friend that, for a marriage to succeed, neither the guys face nor bio data is relevant. Only the woman in question has the right to decide if he is to *her* liking and expectations, or not – and if she has spent enough time getting to know him in misery, anger and happiness. It's a major life decision, not a one-day photoshoot where you see a picture and a bio data and make a decision. This is something on which the next 70-80 years of her life will depend and it requires her participation.

To this she responded, "my uncle has a good sense of understanding men. Even my friend (the so-called engineer) got married without ever speaking to her husband, because they were too shy to talk. Her father made the decision, and her husband is a good boy (sic). The younger sister is even shyer.

Their father has visited sixty homes in the last two months and selected this guy so clearly he *must* be suitable!"

Wow. Sixty homes! I bet people don't work as hard and visit sixty offices in two months for employment. Kudos to her dad. For those who aren't familiar with this culture, let me break down for you how this works.

The first thing in a guy that they see is his surname. If it's a different caste, then he is an alien and instantly rejected.

The second thing they look for is his financial stability. The wealthier, the better. Who cares if in future he treats your daughter like a maid? At least she'll be a maid-cum-wife in a palace.

The third thing is education. For educated families that hang out in matrimonial websites and are aware of how the Internet works, the more degrees beside a guy's name, the more reputation it builds while bragging to neighbours and relatives later at the wedding ceremony.

Forth is his age, family, and house. His age could be anywhere between 20-80, but if he is ultra rich he has a higher chance. His family members *must* have degrees, cars and houses so reputation building again comes easily. The more fame in the community and city, the more social applause will be forthcoming. If the house is fancy, it's great. If not, then the woman's father starts picturing how much money to spend in order to fit their daughter into that house with all the furniture and electronics.

FACEPALM!

65% of Indian women are literate and only a tiny, pathetic, measly 5% have control over choosing their husband.

Aren't I just lucky to be in that measly 5%? Because if I were in that 95%, you wouldn't be reading this book. That I can say with certainty.

Sources:

http://riceinstitute.org/blog/reporting-in-hindu-bbc-and-scroll-on-under-reporting-of-violence-against-women/

http://www.huffingtonpost.com/entry/india-marital-rape_us_564d8c21e4b00b7997f9469e

http://www.thehindu.com/data/statistics-on-marital-rape/article6586829.ece

https://scroll.in/article/829205/80-indian-women-need-permission-to-visit-health-centre-5-have-sole-control-over-choice-of-husband

http://www.hindustantimes.com/india-news/65-indian-women-are-literate-5-have-control-over-choosing-their-husband/story-kymC8H2BKA0hp2D5RiHBdL.html

Chapter 9

—·——✦——·—

The Loyal Daughters of Patriarchy

In India, we have a Hindi phrase called *Abla Naari*, which translates into English as *helpless woman*. As a feminist, I have seen women with a lot of privileges, and those with very few. However I would never say that a woman, in general, is helpless simply because of her gender.

Patriarchy enforces such ignorant beliefs among us, stereotyping woman as 'the weaker sex'. The truth is that women are equally as vulnerable and *powerful* as men. While India has shamefully won the title of being the least safe country in the world for women, it isn't just men that should be forced to shoulder the blame for this embarrassment.

For most women, it is easier to blame men for all kinds of violence and act like victims – or arguably even worse, perpetual *potential* victims. Shockingly, the role of women in uplifting patriarchy and oppression is never talked discussed.

So, how do (many) women contribute to violence against women?

Here are 3 reasons no one wants to admit or talk about.

1. Patriarchal Parenting

In India, women are the primary parent in most households. While they have a perfect opportunity to raise their children as open-minded individuals, they rarely do so. Their parenting includes gender stereotyping which limits the potential of their children to their gender.

If you are a girl, don't go out and play sports. If you are a boy, don't show your emotions or take an interest in the kitchen. Be dirty, lazy and lay around the couch watching TV while your sister cleans up after you; that's your birthright, my son. The limits to young women, meanwhile, are endless. Girls are taught to grow up and study *just enough* to find a suitable husband when the moment comes.

It's the mother who can teach her little girl to dream and fly in the sky, or just do the laundry and dishes. It's also the mother who can teach her boy to respect his sister and friends, while ensuring he is given nothing more than what is offered to his sister. I'm not ignoring the role of men here, but I prefer to write about that in depth in a different article.

For now, it is important to focus on how many opportunities women have in their hands but choose to blissfully ignore because *they themselves* believe in the hardcore gender stereotypes and boundaries defined by society.

2. The Illusion of a Happy Marriage

While many women are facing domestic violence at home, not every woman finds her life threatened or endangered. However, many women face emotional and psychological abuse throughout each moment of their day. They may be educated, hail from well-to-do families and live with educated husbands. They *choose* abuse because they think that being submissive is the key to a happy marriage. Now, I know many of you would do the #whyIstayed reasoning...and I respect all that. However, if you think that acting like a maid is marriage, and you force other women to live like that, you need to broaden your thinking.

What such women fail to realize is that a subject-object relationship is light years away from the word 'marriage'. Women convince themselves – and force other women to believe that suffering and mental stress is an essential element of marriage. I agree that marriage is hard work, and it certainly requires a lot of compromise, but letting another person abuse you is neither. Take a stand for your rights, or simply decline to act like a maid or servant. Cooking and cleaning your husband's dirt, and treating him like an overgrown spoilt baby, is how women raise a man-child husband.

Sharing household chores is a major point of disaster in many Indian marriages, where men take the back seat and women allow them to do so. Those men who *do* share household responsibilities raise better children, who become more mature individuals and succeed in all facets of life.

3. Men as a Personal ATM

Many Indian households prohibit women from working, and what's more, many women do not *want* to work themselves.

Educated women look for financially strong men for marriage (without considering their personalities) just so they can be financially richer. Status and wealth are the most powerful things in the minds of our society and to reach that high, women begin to consider men as their personal ATMs.

Women can, and must, be responsible for their own expenses. In cases where men do not allow them to step out of the house, there is little room for negotiation. However, in many cases I have witnessed, women choose not to work and toil. Instead, they prefer watching saas-bahu daily soaps all day, cooking and cleaning a little, and spending their entire lives complaining about their husbands or parents. Please note that I am *not* discrediting housewives. I actually think that it's the hardest job in the world. But this is about housewives thinking that working women are sluts (used for lack of better word, and to quote the exact term I hear). It is not about who works harder, it is about judging working women and their morality.

A man expressing violence against women is very visible because we see the scars and bruises. Emotional and psychological abuse is actually more prevalent than physical abuse, but is rarely recognised. However, the mental stress that our men face in this harsh world leaves no mark. Men are forced to be the sole breadwinners of their families. The day a baby girl is born, their life is doomed. All they see in that little angel is the pressure of dowry. This is the sole reason for infanticide in India.

Thus, both as fathers and as husbands, men face a lot injustice. Women cannot always change things, but in many cases they can. They *choose* not to, because they are too lazy to step out of the house – and they consider it as beneath them to work for a living. They look down upon women who spend all day in an office and work hard to make their wages.

The most dangerous outcome of this mentality is gender inequality. When feminists oppose patriarchy, they do not *support* matriarchy. At least, that is not what the progressive ones do. Unfortunately, Indian lawmakers, and society in general, do not understand gender equality – even in it's most basic form. To fight patriarchy, they would blindly support matriarchy. We cannot put our sons in danger to save our daughters, and vice versa. I am a hardcore feminist and I support women's rights at the core of my heart, but I do not solely blame men for female oppression.

Feminism stands for gender equality and justice, and that is what India needs. Blind support of either sex is counter-progressive and will lead to more violent crimes and hatred in the hearts of both men and women. Gender equality is not preference of one sex over another; it means treating all genders as equal, and justice for all.

Chapter 10

The Rebellion Against Arranged Marriage

The 'institution of Indian arranged marriage' is more likely to kill a woman than a road accident, malaria, cancer, thunder, shark attack and war combined.

CORE LESSON – Women need to have *a say* in one of the biggest decisions of their life. A say that isn't an outcome of emotional blackmail, guilt, shame or societal pressures.

If you are an Indian woman in your late 20s, you may discover that all of a sudden you have become a thorn in the eye for most of the people around you. From family members to community members, the only question you're likely to hear is. "why aren't you married yet?"

This question is also peppered with pity; pity for your worthlessness, and worry for your unborn children. I was soooooooo pressured by one aunt to hand her my matrimonial bio data, I ultimately made one that you can read on my blog, entitled *Finding Me a Husband.*

I am aware that men also go through this strange phase of being the subject of community and family worry, yet the pressure on women is beyond comparison. My parents are asked questions when are they marrying me off, which silences my existence. I am not an object to be passed from one home to another without a say.

When it comes to marriages in India, the most common notion is that if you marry out of love – meaning as a result of your own choice – you are on your own. In some extreme cases, you even risk being killed, or at best shunned by society. The chaste, moral, traditional, cultural and non-threatening way to marry is a marriage 'arranged' by your parents.

The Role of Parents

I am a firm believer of loving your parents to death. I would sell my kidney for their sake, if need be. Yet, I don't I want them to choose my life partner. Here's why...

1. Placing Parents on a Worship Pedestal

Traditional Indian culture and religious education places utmost importance upon respect of parents and teachers in our society. As we grow up, we are taught to be almost blind to our parent's errors. For an Indian child, his or her parents are next to God; they never err!

This is where the problem lies. Respecting humans is a virtue enough; placing them on a pedestal next to God is unnecessary and exaggerating. The fact is, they are human and, as a result, make as many mistakes as any other person. Just because they are your parents, you are programmed to be blind to their wrongdoings. This is not about blaming parents; it's about realising where their mentality and ideology is coming from.

Actually, I think that children being critical of their parents is a necessary developmental step. When a child asks her parent to stop smoking, or that he does not want his toys to be bought using black money, this can be extremely helpful.

Returning to the marriage arrangement, don't blindly believe that your parents will choose the best partner out there. They mean well, but never forget that their generation was wildly different from ours.

I imagine that my parents don't even know half the vocabulary I use in my everyday language. I'm not projecting that I'm more cultured or educated; simply stating that patterns of conversation, the ways we behave, our psychology, our attitudes... *everything* has wildly changed in the last couple of decades. Your parents may want the best for you according to *their* intentions, yes, but the outcome may not necessarily be helpful to you.

2. Most Parents Favour Dowry

For instance, I completely oppose dowry. My mother, meanwhile, considers it to be a cultural obligation that's required to sustain a marriage. In other words, it's the price we pay to buy your happiness and rights as a wife in your husband's home. I, on the other hand, feel that if my husband marries me based on material things, what sort of a superficial fake relationship it would be? So, women must *buy* respect and rights by offering hefty dowries? Do they come with a 5-year warranty that he will treat me like a human? Is there a No-Questions-Asked return policy?

3. Excessive Moral Policing on Young People's Choices

Many of my friends, even those who married out of love, ended up telling everyone around that it was an arranged marriage. The words 'love marriage' were shameful, and spoiled their moral or cultural reputation in a community that demands youths to be chaste and pious; by choosing your life partner, you somehow become a skank. Many marriages fall apart, but when a love marriage falls apart the immediate blame is placed at the feet the bride for choosing the wrong guy, hurting her parents, and stepping out of line. When an arranged marriage falls apart, the blame isn't placed upon the parents for choosing the wrong guy. It's simply tagged as a 'gamble of destiny'.

4.   Parent's Choose the Best Myth

Many of the supporters of this arranged marriage argue that they rely on their parents to choose what's best for them. I think that if you are not mature enough to decide what is best for you, you are not mature enough to handle the responsibility of a relationship.

If you cannot decide which person is best for you, why the hell are you getting married? And even if your parents choose for you, how long are you exactly going to rely on them to make your life decisions for you?

Most people argue that their parents should choose their life partners because they want the best for their children. I agree that parents want the best for their kids, but just the *intention* of wanting the best is not enough for me. I know that my parents want the best for me, but they are *not* me. I'm not my mother, neither am I my father. My ideals and values are different from those of my parents. Their values and ideas are defined by their generation, and mine are defined by the world I see around me.

5.   Both Partners Role in Understanding Marriage

Unlike what the thick glossy magazines tell you, a marriage is more than flowers, cake, dresses and jewellery. It's about the hardship of being under the same roof with another person. Sharing your body, your space, time and *life* with this person. Would you call your parents every time you have an argument over which drawer the socks go in? Why can't we raise our children to understand relationships deeper than exchanging things, and being responsible for their behaviour instead of being an unwanted referee in their lives? The nose of a third party between couples is never a good idea, unless it's a case of domestic violence and professional help is needed.

6. Mama's Boy Tales

I recently rejected a guy who wanted to marry me 'arranged fashion'. The reason why I rejected him was that his placenta seemed to be perfectly intact, still. Many people call such guys 'a mama's boy'!

I mean, I am expected to leave my parents and family behind even though I am five years younger, and the guy has all the right to cling to his mommy for the rest of our married life?

My problem here is not that the guy loves his family. I love my family too. However, I am also a grown-up woman, and I know that when I get married, I'll start another family – my own. I continue to remain a part of the old family tree, but I become a primary starter of a new branch. Indian men, however, largely fail to see a distinction between the two families. I partially blame society for this notion, as whenever a man grows closer to marriage, his friends and siblings begin to bully him about being 'joru ka ghulam' – which means *a servant of the wife*.

This particular guy I am talking about was so afraid of these comments that, when it came to discuss marriage, all I heard from him was how important *his* family was to him. He never mentioned how he was looking forward to beginning *our* family. There was nothing about me other than being an outsider who had to try and 'fit in' with his family. Why was everything just about his family, his parents, and his life? Where did I fit into all this?

Now, I know that I am unconventional and I do not follow the lame excuse of 'culture' in most references. I have simple rules. If a man wants to marry me, he has to begin the conversation as *us* meaning he and I, instead of *us* referring to his parents, siblings, their spouses and kids, and then maybe – if there is any time and energy left – me. I don't understand why it is forced and considered natural for a woman to abandon her family and her love for her siblings, while the guy is supposed to keep those relationships at high priority?

Arranged marriages are *this* institution of oppression, where the role of a woman is confined to being a maid, servant or babymaker. FYI, this also happens in love marriages, where the balance of power in the relationship is unhealthy and the woman is forced by her husband to 'win the hearts' of his family members. Many women complain how their boyfriends made terrible husbands.

7. Other Reasons for 'Arranging Marriages' between Families

It's not just about two families exchanging wealth in return of selling their son. There's a lot going on undercover, and parents willingly put up their girls through the following –

- Underage girls put up for marriages.

- Girls forced into marriages to settle family dealings.

- Girls never allowed to meet and or talk to the guy they're expected to marry.

- Pure economical exchange of a dowry and virginal woman.

- Girls married off just to advertise an image in the community.

- Educational and career opportunities of girls are killed.

Now, ask yourself – do you think that *these* girls don't have parents? Do you think that *all* parents want the best of their children?

Now, I know there are a lot of people out there that may have found this chapter offensive. You may be one them, thinking of how you are living a perfectly contented life as part of an arranged marriage. If that's the case, I'm genuinely happy for you – but this article is not about you, is it?

This is about those who suffer because they do not want to disappoint their parents. Those who were married off and told that, "a woman goes to her husband's home in doli and only comes out in a coffin."

Arranged marriages elsewhere in the world – as in blind dating, or dates arranged by friends and family – are completely different from the Indian practice of arranged marriages *because of the right to say no, and the freedom to say yes depending on their own choices.* The destiny of any child should not be the decision of their parents from the moment they reach adulthood.

I love and respect my parents with all my heart but my husband has no existence in my heart if I didn't choose him for myself. I he is chosen by others and I'm forced to love him, how would he ever feel proud that his wife chose him?

Chapter 11

⸺⸺✈⸺⸺

The Hush Hush Things They Will Never Talk About

Trigger warning: this chapter is all about self-harm, depression, suicide and mental illness in general. If this kind of content triggers any issues with you, please refrain from reading.

I remember it like it happened yesterday.

I stared at the razor like it was an angel that could grant me a wish.

Sitting at my dad's office desk, knowing it was locked inside, I could think of nothing else but this razor. The razor my Dad would use to slit envelopes, or sharpen a wooden pencil. And now it was my respite.

As I continued staring at the shiny silver razor, sadness rolled down my despairing swollen eyes. You might be thinking what could possibly lead a teenager to think of self-harming?

As the voices in my head got louder I picked up the razor with my right hand and tested its sharpness by slightly scratching the back of my hand. The instantly ripped skin was evidence the razor was in perfect condition. Unlike me.

It took me two hours or more to go through with it. But finally, in one moment, it happened. I tightened my wrist like it was holding onto life itself, and held the razor at a right angle with the right hand. I didn't want to die, and I wanted the scars to be hidden. As a result, the perfect place to slit was the area adjacent to the wrist.

Being a Highly Sensitive Person (HSP) I didn't have the courage to keep my eyes open. I turned my head, screwed my eyes shut as tight as my wrist, and in one motion dragged the silver blade across my wrist towards the arm. To my surprise, I didn't feel anything. I opened my eyes and looked at my newly ripped flesh. Slowly tiny droplets of blood appeared in a straight line, and when there were enough droplets to make an ocean of misery, it slipped over the sides.

It was a strange moment; one that felt weak and courageous at the same time. Weak, because it felt cowardly to hurt myself like this. Courageous, because it gave me some sense of *control*. Years later, I learned that this behaviour is done as a coping mechanism for someone wanting to feel a sense of control.

I also learned that that day, when I was slitting my wrist locked inside my dad's office, that I wasn't alone.

There were many others like me. In fact, there were *millions of* others.

India alone accounts for approximately 30 per cent of the world's suicide deaths. In 2013, suicide claimed the lives of more than a quarter of a million Indians. That's five times greater than all global deaths due to war and natural disasters combined.[1] And these are the people that didn't just slit a part of them like me; these people actually succeeded in ending their lives, full and final.

If you have never been sad or depressed or don't *get* why someone would do such a thing, I have got things to tell you. And please don't start with the, "just get over it, life is unfair, have you tried positive thinking, look how ungrateful you are, just take a walk, you are crazy, overacting, bla bla bla" speech – we've all heard it before, and it has helped precisely nobody.

I had all the symptoms; panic, anxiety, self-harm and depression. Yet, despite living right under their noses, my family members didn't see it. It all began with a guy. A guy I had nothing to do with, or was never interested in either. A guy that took it upon himself to beat up some other guys who catcalled me on the street. In Chapter 12 I discuss this further – how men harass you themselves, but are super protective when the other guy does it.

So, this guy was chasing me for months, and he maintained his attempts to woo me. As he lived close by, one day, on the street he saw some random guys on a bike, passing by my side and spitting some bullshit as guys do. I was gone and unaware of what was to come.

This Romeo beat up those two guys, who later returned with fifteen friends to return the compliment, beating this guy

[1] http://www.humanosphere.org/global-health/2016/08/suicide-deaths-india-increasing-alarming-rate/

and his brother so badly they had to go to the ER. Later that night, someone called and I learned about the whole thing. Now, I don't know how, but *somehow* I was the one to blame.

I was already struggling with this notion that the guy was calling me and blaming that it all happened because of me when something else happened. Since my neighbourhood is a close-knit community, everybody's nose is in other peoples business. Ergo, the rumours began.

A friend of mine dropped by and informed me that an elderly woman in the neighbourhood was spreading rumours about the guy and me; something nasty. I can't recall *exactly* what because, by the time she reached that part, I was already nauseated. As soon as she left, I had a severe panic attack – I couldn't breathe at all. My mom heard my throat fighting for air and came to help. Due to lack of oxygen, I think, my vision blackened and I felt like a heavy stone being placed at the centre of my forehead. It's a weird feeling. It feels like something has sucked your soul through a pipe fitted right at the centre of your forehead, and as it sucks your life away, before your hands and feet grow so cold that you lose all mobility and sense from your body.

I was immediately hospitalised and rehabilitated through an oxygen mask. It was boiling hot that June, and the private rooms in the hospital were all taken. This was my first experience in a hospital in India, and it was *ugly*. The nurses had zero humanity and the place was like a diseased, overcrowded factory. A few days later I was taken to a private room when a cancer patient died. What luck!

There was no sign of recovery in me, and by now I had a consistently high fever that wasn't dropping despite intravenous antibiotics being injected into me day and night. I wasn't eating anything, and my only source of energy was a glucose drip. I had my eyes closed most of the time, and had zero energy to even talk. During the few minutes that my thought processes would come to life, the only thing I could think of was shame, guilt and sorrow.

You see, if you still didn't get it, the moral policeman that my mother had planted in my head during childhood was in full power. According to him, my worth, my self respect and my life was attached to a word called honour, and this honour was something I was entrusted to protect by my mother. All through school, I never had a fling with any guy, only and only because, "nice girls don't have boyfriends". The thought of people talking about Mr. Khan's daughter doing something shameful was so powerful, it was slowly killing me.

Now, upon reflection, I wonder about the role others played in my chronic depression. How the doctors asked me if I was holding something in me that was hampering my recovery. The role the Romeo played in harassing me for weeks and refusing to take no for an answer. The role that neighbourhood women played in creating slut shaming stories about me, and other people's daughters. The role my friend played in telling me about it, and the role my mother played in making me believe that other people's opinions matter more than me. That the so-called badge of honour she placed on me was more important than her own little girls life.

I wish that I could blame nobody but myself, but I cant ignore the role society played in making me think that a rumour has more worth than my life.

One miserable evening in the hospital, my aunt came to visit me. It was the 15th day, and my body was lifeless; my eyes were closed, and my veins were swollen and so blocked with antibiotics that the nurses were pushing the blobs of that liquid with their thumbs into my veins. While my dad sat next to me, narrating my condition to his sister, he cried!

I felt the tremors of a massive earthquake in my soul. For a girl, her father is her ultimate source of strength; the man who protects her, holds her, saves her from monsters in her nightmares and lifts her up before she hits rock bottom. This unfortunate day, that strong as a pyramid figure in my life, my father, *cried*! As motionless and limp as my body was after 15 days of no solid food and water, I somehow got up and sat on my own and hugged him. As I write this today, in 2017 almost 13 years later, my throat has a lump and my eyes are as wet as Niagara Falls.

There was no therapy, no mental health experts and no healing. Not because I didn't want it, simply cause nobody offered, and I didn't know it existed to ask for it.

That one moment put a giant boulder in my path towards destruction and self-pity lane. I realised that if I was prepared to die for a pathetic stranger, why wouldn't I live for the man I love most in the world? Actually, I wasn't even planning to die. It was a weird stage where you do not voluntarily kill yourself, but you lose the will to live – and maybe you just don't know how to. You grow too focused on that one pang of a toxic person that you forget you have a life to live, and people to love. And my dad's tears were the electric shock that brought back my sinking pulse to life.

It was a decision I made, and things began to change. That one long, tight hug in my dad's arms told me that, no matter what the world says or does, my life means something and I cant let it suffer; because when I suffer, my dad suffers. Within four days, I was out of that hospital. While at home, I was still prescribed medication and bed rest for a month. I had a changed mindset and a new vision on life.

It's not that I never got sad in my life, or never faced depression. I still do now, but I handle it well enough that it does not reach my family. Since leaving home in 2007, I went through a myriad of life experiences, some of which were so painful that I won't bother writing them at this moment. Yet my family knows nothing of this. I simply *can't* put my parents through it. I have to protect them from my demons, and the monsters that chase me.

Pain is an inevitable part of life, and everybody has their own way of dealing with it. Mental illnesses such as panic, anxiety, posttraumatic stress disorder and chronic depression are manifestations of that pain. And you and I can only decide the pain and its degree for our own individual selves. The stupidest thing in the world is to judge another persons pain and say, "oh *that's* nothing."

Therefore, self-harm became a coping mechanism. Once, when my mother *did* see the scars, I made an excuse that it was accidental while working with envelopes. She gave me a weird look. I don't know if that look was the one that parents give to their children when they catch them in the act of doing something secretive. Or was it the look of frustration that said, "I believe you, but why can't you be more careful?" I don't know, because we never talked about it. She never asked if I was going though something, and I never had the words or the courage to express what I felt in words that she could understand.

Regardless, mental health issues in our homes are less talked about than ghosts. Indian parents believe ghosts exist, but not mental health issues. The only mental health issue they consider important enough to seek professional help for is when one completely loses their memory, logic and understanding abilities.

There's so much stigma attached to depression and other related things, they pretend it doesn't exist. It's just *easier* that way. Recently, I watched *13 Reasons Why* on Netflix and it brought up a lot of emotional trauma for me. I have been feeling tipped off ever since it ended. I am not blaming the show, don't get me wrong; it is something every single person must see to understand what its like inside the mind of someone that kills themself. And I loved the way the writers and directors made the transition from the before and after parts of her life. How everyone she sought help from brushed her feelings under the carpet.

The 1st of March is celebrated as Self Injury Awareness Day, and this year I was invited to Cardiff Radio to speak about the issue. It was terrifying for me to talk about my secret that I had been hiding under long sleeves since forever in public, on a freaking radio station. But I did it, and I did it with pride rather than shame. Pride that I may be helping other people *not* to repeat the same mistake I did; of worrying about what other people thought before myself. The self-harm I inflicted upon my arm was the policeman in my head telling me that I deserved to be punished and suffer pain for unknowingly bringing shame to my family. That policeman is now dead. I killed him because I learned forgiveness for myself. This is where feminism intersects with mental illness.

Everything that I know about depression, self-harm and the background of my own life experience, I found in self-care as preached by feminists.

I learned to value my body, my mind, my choices and the people I love. I learned to talk about everything that was stigmatised and brushed under the carpet. Feminism gave meaning to my actions, and helped me to identify my vulnerabilities while being strong. One of the greatest strengths of the human soul is to admit that they need help, and now I don't feel embarrassed about it. I seek help when it's needed, and I try to learn ways to get that help reach others too. Just as JK Rowling did when she returned to the UK from Portugal after a failed marriage with a newborn baby. She describes that period as the hardest time of her life; she was almost homeless, surviving on benefits, jobless and chronically depressed.

In her Harvard speech, she openly talked about how that stage of her life took the best of her. She was smart enough to seek professional help, and privileged enough to *get* that help. She started spending most of her time writing. She already had the book idea and the plotlines in her mind from much earlier, but never before had she found the time and inclination to write her books with utmost concentration. Her depression was eating away at her bit by bit when she started writing, and expressing her feelings was a respite. She was rejected by ten major publishers before her first book ever saw daylight. Today she has sold more than 400 million books of her *Harry Potter* series, but it was the seeking of professional help at the right time that saved her from chronic depression and suicidal thoughts.

A teenager in Mumbai recently filmed his suicide on Facebook LIVE. Clearly, depression and sadness has its pangs in our youth digging deeper. And as a society, maybe talking about it instead of pretending it doesn't exist would be much better. Prince William and Lady Gaga recently had a LIVE chat about mental health issues that went viral. She suffered from PTSD after a rape, and Prince William was keen on the trauma of bereavement after his mother Princess Diana's untimely death. While many sympathised with this courage of announcing her PTSD publically, a handful of others like Piers Morgan called it 'vain-glorious nonsense'. And this is why women, specifically, don't talk about their traumatic experiences or their impact.

It takes unimaginable amounts of guts to end your life. It's the only one you have, after all, and the only thing that makes you *you*. It takes even more courage to have suicidal thoughts and decide to choose life and raise awareness about it. I hear people say if you are sad and think about ending your life that you should find what makes you happy, find something to look forward to, and something to do on a daily basis. J.K Rowling found writing. She looked forward to that, and it made her happy.

Despite me talking about self-harm and suicidal thoughts publically, and helping others avoid my mistakes, I am still a work in progress. I am in no position to claim that I will never battle mental illness again. See, its like an uninvited guest in your mind; you can never say when it will be back. Especially with PTSD – you never know when a memory will be triggered, and you will receive a flashback of something you do your best to repress in your mind. It still happens, but I found what makes me *happy* and that's what brings me back to life – making others smile. It may sound hooey and mushy, but when a stranger from oceans away tells you that you made an impact and saved them from making the biggest mistake of their life, it means a lot.

What I do with specific people will not be published in newspapers, it wont go viral on the Internet, and you will never hear songs about my name or deeds. It's personal to the person that I helped, and their stories are just theirs. What's mine is just the relief that one life has breathed easier because of me. And that is my inspiration for survival. Who, or what, do *you* live for?

On this journey of self-discovery, I also made another life altering revelation about my own self. I am a Highly Sensitive Person. Dr Elane Aron's empirical research uncovered this special gene that almost 20% of the world population has. People with a genetic trait of sensory processing sensitivity.

Highly Sensitive People

HSPs have some very evident life experiences that are particularly true in my case.

- My mind doesn't switch off. I have regular problems with sleeping, not least because my brain is like an Internet browser with 157 windows open at any given time.

- Graphic violence imagery haunts me forever. Since my childhood, I could never watch horror movies.

- I can't sleep in just any bed; I have very specific requirements. Things have to be just right, just the way I am used to in my own bed.

Regardless, I love that I strongly, deeply connect with others, being a HSP.

Some other Core traits of HSPs are:

- **Depth of processing** – we analyse everything deeply. So next time you say to a HSP, "ah relax, you're overthinking it" – yes, we are. And there's nothing we can do about that.

- **Overstimulation** – the world around us quickly overwhelms us.

- **Empathy** – when one cries, the other tastes salt

- **Awareness of subtleties** – we pick up on the smallest things. We may wake you at 3am to tell you about the tap flowing two floors down.

There's a common stereotype that HSPs but must simply be introverts, but 30% of HSPs are actually extroverts. Because of the traits, people assume all HSPs are women but 50% of HSP are men. Sadly, men that can be both sensitive and strong are too alien a concept for the world.

I see myself that I am one of those people whose senses are heightened and experiences can be overwhelming, I see why so many things that happened had such an impact on me. I see why it is so easy for the handful of people I love to hurt me so easily and deeply.

Relationships for a HSP

Hundreds of people ask me why am I not married already. Having a past that includes depression and being an extremely sensitive person, marriage for me is a greater risk than it is to others. For a simple example – I have a cousin who has an abusive husband. Instead of standing up to him and sorting her troubles, she prefers to talk about their issues and flirt with other men when he isn't around. Not just about the abuse, but intimate issues and private things to whomever she can on her side of the family. She clearly says she does not love the man and is pushing the marriage as a compromise because she is too 'respectable' to get a divorce. The *married* tag is more important to her. So be it!

I would have done things very differently. I would never have talked behind my husband's back to others. I would never be with a man I do not love with all my heart, never make a circus out of my intimate secrets with my husband, and never stay in a marriage for showing off to society that I am a successful wife.

Yes, I empathise with people, and sadly that includes people who do me wrong. I'd rather stay single than enter into a relationship with the wrong man and then fake happiness until till eternity.

You might as well call me weak and fearful, but I just think it is a coping mechanism. A survival strategy to avoid placing myself in situations that I do not see myself feeling completely honest and happy in.

I don't take marriage vows lightly. I have not married yet, and when I do decide to marry, I intend to keep my promises. If, for whatever reason, I would feel that isn't possible, I would back out to their face, not talk behind their back.

But again, that's just me.

I Can't Give You Me

I can't give you me

As much as I love love

As much as I want to be loved

I cant' give you me.

To the world I am a strong woman

I am the cliff that men train to hike,

I am the oak tree that stands after the hurricane,

I am the earth that lies beneath your feet

And you think you can walk all over it

But the moment it shakes you are wiped out

Like a tiny speck on the face of the moon.

I am Maya Angelou's phenomenal woman

I am the one that gives Trump nightmares,

The one that were once tagged as witches

And in some centuries, the suffragettes.

To the world, I am all that.

But to the man I love, not that at all.

When I am in love,

I am like the drop of wax slowly and gracefully,

Trembling down the lengths of a candle,

Warm but soft and crushed by the tip of the mans finger.

As a woman in love,

I am the tiny speck hiding in the pollen of a sunflower,

As the sun gives it light, so it owns the power to burn it.

Love makes me care, love makes me give you my all,

And if I give you me, I will love you that way.

Love you more than you ever imagined and

Be there for you more than you deserve.

Going an extra mile after 5000 extra miles is my thing.

Unlucky for you, I have been there done that.

Travelled those miles, been crushed and burnt and broken.

Now, when you say the word love,

I hear my bones cracking like you've already started

To tighten your grip on my fragility

And when you say 'commitment'

I feel my existence withering away in gray ashes.

And when you say 'relationship'

I crumble like a hard rock sliding down a cliff.

It's not you, it's those words.

Those exact words men used before you and

That makes me wonder

Why would you be any different.

I know its foolish to give up on love.

As they say, when one bus goes...

But what if the buses keep coming but none of them is the right one.

I may sound like a coward to you,

Like a hopeless, powerless, weak woman.

Too afraid to put herself out there.

Too scared to just 'get on with life'.

The fact is- I am different.

I have a history and I have been at places you cannot imagine.

When I love someone, I give them a weird sense of control over me.

I swear its not voluntary, its like air.

People have used that to my disadvantage very well.

To humiliate me, harass me, crush me and dehumanize me.

And now that I know how delicate it is,

I rather guard it myself.

You are human after all, and I am afraid,

Knowingly or unknowingly if someday

You decide to use it as a weapon on me,

I may not find back the strength

To put the pieces back together,

Not all broken mirrors can be fixed.

Sometimes the shards are too sharp and cut too deep.

Chapter 12

———— ⚜ ————

The Moral Policeman My Mom Planted in My Head

I say police*man* and not woman because, from what the person said, the voice seemed more masculine and patriarchal in tone. The voice said things that sounded distinctly male, telling me things that a man would benefit from.

Shockingly enough they came from the mouth of my mother. Maybe she is his secret agent? Who knows. Regardless, here's what the voice talks about.

- Thou shall not wear perfume, because not only living men but male ghosts will be attracted to you and start following you.

- Don't let thine hair down outside, especially not in the garden, a public place or anywhere where a cool breeze could make you give the pleasure of liberation for even one second. The reasons are the same as the above.

- While going out of the house, thou shall make sure:

    - it's not dark outside, because the needles of a watch decide your character.

    - it's a safe enough time of the day, season and year; festival season is off-limits.

    - you have a company with you – never go alone.

    - you have covered your body enough to be tagged as a decent woman.

- When thou *are* outside, if a loafing sleazeball brushes off against you, it is *always* your fault for letting him do that and, by default, just being in his way.

- Thou shall not visit graveyards because dead bodies see living women naked. Nobody ever explained how they know this. I mean, unless someone from the other side came back and told them about it, how would you know? And why only men see women naked? What about seeing other men naked? You don't think ghosts can be gay? I often try to envision how would that conversation go.

Ghost: "ahem, excuse me hottie."

Shocked woman: "who are you?"

Ghost: "Madam, I'm the soul from that ditch on the left. You see, you are not supposed to be here. My friends and I can see you nude through our x-ray vision and honestly, you are distracting us".

Woman, now more shocked: "Distracting you? From what?"

Ghost: Deep sigh [-------------------------]

Woman, now feisty: "And how come you find me distracting but not l seeing all the men nude? I smell some homo interests..."

Ghost: "Madam, please carry on."

- Any adolescent girl who gains weight and develops fuller hips is an indication of them having a lot of sex. I checked, and this is scientifically inaccurate. If anything, having sex means burning a lot of calories, and therefore no connection can be made between weight gain and having pre-marital sex.

- Men are all dogs (oh, the irony), so never ever ever *ever* trust any man, no matter how sure thou may be of his intentions. All men are dirty, disgusting, potential rapists. And if he does rape you, it's *always* your fault for trusting him and thinking he is a human.

- Do not use tampons, because they take thine virginity – that is the right that belongs to your future – obviously a stranger, and male, but in this case not a dog and a rapist because we chose him for you – husband alone. If you are a non-virgin, you become worthless as a human.

- Thine body is a moving, living, breathing embodiment of your family's honour and respect in society. Anything you do with your body has a direct impact on the honour and respect your family has in society.

- Yes, daughters are great and we are all for female empowerment, but only as long as women behave themselves; wear what we say is appropriate; do what we say; marry wealthy, unloving husbands; and pump out babes like a vending machine. Only *those* daughters are great. The rest, we don't like to talk about. Lets just bury them, figuratively.

- Sons are nice too, but as long as they become doctors or engineers; marry women we choose for them; and, no matter how unhappy they be, just keep sending us money as your responsibility towards your parents.

- No matter how much thou shall earn, as a son or daughter, your parents will always find someone who earns more than you and it is their holy right to harass and humiliate you that you aren't earning as much as the neighbour's kid.

- If someone's *son* has travelled abroad to make a life, he must be working hard to make a future. If someone's *daughter*_has travelled abroad, she certainly must be selling herself on the streets, or has become a white man's mistress.

- If thou are over 22 and single, you either must be ugly; have a dark complexion; your parents lack the wealth for a hefty dowry; or be diseased, mentally ill, or had pre-marital sex. There is no reason you could be *normal* and choose to stay single until you make your career, or decide which guy you want to marry.

- Bra straps are a complete no-no. The world must not know thou have a bra on. It's shameful; hide it. Weapons of Mass Destruction in Iraq can be found but not your bra straps.

- If you wish to keep thine husband, be his mother in the kitchen, sister when you go out, and prostitute in bed. If you don't you will lose him to another woman and nobody would be to blame but yourself.

- Thou just can't let yourself go. Men are visual creatures; they don't care about your loyalties, and care for them. As long as you keep a tiny waist, a flawless skin with foundation on, a body shaven as smooth as that of a baby and be on your toes 24/7, your husband will be happy. Probably. Kind of.

- Thou can never earn more than your husband. It will bruise his male ego, and we can't risk *that*. You better dumb down your brain, but let him feel proud of his mediocrity.

- Live-in relationships? Thou want to be stoned to death?

- Consent is all this modern fake crap polluting the minds of women. There's no such thing as consent. Once you marry a man, you are at his disposal until you die. He deserves orgasms, whether or not you are well, have recently given birth, are aching with menstrual cramps or simply not in the mood. Who cares?

- No matter if thou are a working woman, you must *always* come home before your husband and welcome him home with a hot meal and clean house. It's always *your* job. Who cares if you just tackled a million dollar deal at the office?

- A woman's ultimate ambition is to become a wife and a mother. Who gives a crap if thou are changing the world, writing books, working for the UN or doing whatever it is that makes you happy? Unless you're male-possessed human property and squeeze out his babies, you are not worthy of respect.

- If thine husband beats thou, you must have done something to provoke him. Stay with a wife beater until he becomes a good man (which will never happen). He will just get old and his energies will die out with time.

- As long as thine husband is bringing money home, let him fuck you and be his maid. The second his job is gone, we need to talk about things. Don't worry – this still does not make you a whore, because whores have a choice. You don't.

This is the crap I grew up with. Need I say more?

Chapter 13

———❧———

Marriage Material Women, and Other Hypocrisies of Men

Sana and Salim were watching TV when a song started playing in which Katrina Kaif, the famous Indian actress, was dancing. Salim was instantly drawn to her and admired her sexy figure and the way she looked.

Sana felt a bit uncomfortable, but couldn't say so. She was told men are like 'that'. Having her self-esteem hit by a train, she decided to change something. She decided to start looking after herself and a change few things about the way she dressed. It's not that Salim wasn't attracted to her, but she wanted his eyes to widen and drool the way they did for Katrina.

A few days later, they were about to go for dinner when Katrina decided to surprise him.

She wore a lovely skirt with a body wrap top, and did her hair and makeup properly. She looked radiant and stylish. She did not go out of her way to put on something that would make her uncomfortable and superficial, but something that felt true to her.

As she sprayed the perfume bubbles on her neck, she grabbed her clutch purse and stepped out. In a flirting pose, she stood in the doorway for Salim to notice.

He did. And boy did he.

"What the fuck is that?" he yelled.

"What's wrong?" she trembled.

"Do you expect me to take you out like *this*? Half naked?"

Sana's excitement was ebbing away. More like frozen in shock.

"I am wearing proper clothes, in what way am I naked to your eyes? I just look smart because I am wearing a form fitting, stylish attire and not the garbage sack dress and jacket like everyday".

His voice got harsher and louder.

"Look woman, I am not taking you out looking like a whore. In my world, this is naked, and I want you to go put on something that a modest and respectable woman would wear".

Now it was getting beyond Sana's understanding, and she was boiling inside.

"I used to wear similar clothes when you met me and you never complained back then. When you see these women on TV wearing skimpy clothes you love their attire – you can't stop eye banging them! When your own wife looks smart – not even *sexy*, merely smart and stylish – you humiliate me and say this is not respectful? So, the women on TV you drool over are not respectful? If they aren't, why do you fucking love them so much?"

Sana showed him the mirror and he hated the sight of his hypocritical face. As a result, he did what any other similar man like him does – he grew physically violent and pushed her.

"That's it. Don't talk back to me, you bitch. This is my home and you do what I say. Get the fuck away and cook me dinner. I will never take you out unless you cover yourself and your head".

"Ah, what an evening that was!" Sana says now, as she got free from the shackles of that hypocrite. Sadly enough, this is *not* an isolated event though.

Men have a very different compartment for women they want to marry, a.k.a 'wife material', and desirable women they want to have sex with.

Ever heard of the **Madonna-Whore Complex?**

Nope? Here's what it says.

When I first heard this phrase I initially thought that it looked like something created by *Vogue* or *Cosmopolitan* magazine. It turns out it has more credibility than that. Much more.

The term Madonna-Whore Complex was first coined by the father of Psychoanalysis, Sigmund Freud. The Madonna-Whore Complex is known as the distinction men draw between women they *desire* and women they *respect* – with the implication that those two categories are mutually exclusive.

You remember when someone told you to never tell your husband if you had a past, especially if it was a sexual one? You may think he is a nice guy and all, but you can never mention your past because you are 100% certain that he will judge you and call you a slut/whore for losing your virginity before marriage. This is the Madonna-Whore Complex, where men judge women to be worthy of respect or worthy of sexual desire; not both.

Even married women are expected to act repulsed by sex, never to initiate it. If they initiate sex and express their desires, their husbands instantly tag them as slutty and dislike them being 'whorish', in their words, which is logically just embracing their sexuality.

Sexuality of a woman is a very natural biological urge that does not deserve to be paraded for judgment, yet it is the ultimate basis of a woman's reputation in many societies. So much so that it is used to compartmentalise women. People decide if a woman is marriage material or not.

I don't know to be honest what is their rationale behind it, because to me it's absurd. Yet it certainly *is* a thing if Pippa Middleton got caught into this. Yes, I know this book is about third world women, but apparently there are many absurdities prevalent in the entire world including first world nations.

The Daily Mail reported:

Pippa's 18-month romance with Old Etonian Alex Loudon recently ended because his family considered her not quite 'wife material' — a phrase guaranteed to make female hackles rise. In this supposedly egalitarian age, is there really such a thing as 'wife material'?

If that does not disgust you enough, here is another one.

Psychologist Dr Jane McCartney, an expert in human behaviour and relationships, reports that, "men are attracted to qualities such as loyalty, discretion and kindness when they look for a wife. Feisty and flirty is fine for a girlfriend. It's just not what men want in life partners."

Wow, such noble and crystal clear ideals!

Author Pat Gaudette says it best –

Working through this complex will require that the man change his perceptions of women and his perceptions of the sex act so that he stops putting the label of "whore" on women who are sexually active.

A man diagnosed with the Madonna/Whore Complex does not want to have a wife who is "a lady in public and a whore in the bedroom." He wants his wife to be a lady in public and in the bedroom. He does not want her to be sexually aggressive, or whorish (in his view). He wants her to be pure in mind and body, virginal in every way. For him, love does not equal sex nor does sex equal love.

Wow, such interesting ironies, right? You haven't seen anything yet. Here's another story that will make you want to bitch slap some people; unfortunately it's true, being the tale of the ordeal a friend of mine went through.

Her husband and she were lovers before they got married, which in India is not so common. During their affair, the guy would go nuts to go out for dates and get extremely mad if she did not show up on his clinic every other day (they were both doctors). He would force her to meet him at his home alone when his parents were away, which she claims she never did because she was afraid if she went through with it he would have sex and then break off the wedding deal. God bless these people and their variation on logic.

Finally, after a few months, they were married. She dreamed of a lovely honeymoon destination considering how passionate he was to take her out all the time. She was happier because the guy and his family extorted a car out of the bride's father in the name of dowry, and she planned to drive around several places in the new vehicle.

The first time she asked her newly wedded husband, "what do you say, should we visit the fair in town this evening?" his response couldn't be clearer.

"Fuck off, bitch. Go get me lunch. I will visit the fair with my guy friends and you sit at home, cook dinner and wash dishes for my parents."

The ordeal never ended until her divorce. During their two-year marriage, she asked him several times to go out, visit friends, have dinners, explore some place that could make her *forget* their depressing married life for a few moments. Alas, he stopped even taking her to the clinic. She had to hire a rickshaw and visit the clinic herself if she wanted to. Then he stopped giving her money for transport.

She questioned his behaviour several times, reminding him how he used to be the one that pushed her to meet him outside and now he has completely changed. He had a very typical and weird (for us women only) response that she quotes verbatim -

"You don't date your wife, you date girlfriends. As long as you were my girlfriend, I had to try to please you and chase you. But you are my wife now. Why the fuck do I care to take you out with me? I need to get away from you."

Taking women for granted is something men do excellently, as they have very different profiles of girlfriends, wives and daughters in their minds.

For a woman, she would love a man who is like her father and would feel proud if her son is like his father.

Men, on the other hand, seek an attractive wife – just not *too* sexy, as that would be just a girlfriend and not 'marriage material'. When it comes to daughters they want them to be super geeky and average so other boys don't pursue them. They want their daughters to be strong and independent, actually even smarter than their mothers, but not physically attractive, according to The Shriver Report.

I have never ever heard a woman say that she does wants her son to look ugly on purpose. Neither do they wish for their daughters to be ugly and unattractive. I suppose men have inside information about other men, hence they don't want other men to do to *their* daughter what they did to someone *else's* daughter.

If you are a fan of *The Big Bang Theory*, the famous American sitcom, you may be familiar with an episode where Howard and Raj are in a car, discussing the gender of Howard's upcoming child. And Howard gets worried and fears what if she is a girl ... because you know how guys are with girls.

Howard's character has been the creepiest all through the series, and now he is worried that if he has daughter, other guys would be mean and creepy to her. His hypocrisy is seen in another episode when him and Raj are redecorating Howard's old room into a nursery for baby Haley. In a moment Howard reminisces how he grew up in that room and how much sex he had there and speaking the same for his daughter, he creeps out. Just the thought of his daughter having a sexually active life just breaks his conversation like thunder and lightening. But I guess a son with a sexually active life is a stud and a charmer?

We are in the 21st century and in every country in the world, a man's sexuality is the proof of his prowess and a woman's sexuality is a damper on not just her reputation, but her worth as a human being. We are sending humans on Mars but we cannot admit that women have biological urges just like men.

Reena shares her story that is weird AF. She was sharing a house with some people, one of whom she considered a good friend. One night they were watching TV and before she left he said he would rub her shoulders, as she seemed tense. Despite a thousand declinations he kept insisting and made a promise that it would be nothing else.

Of course it was a manipulation for sex. It led to, "I will only kiss and stop". Then, "I will only caress you and stop."

He did not stop.

Trusting her friend, and shocked by what was happening, she froze. She could not come to terms with what happened. After the rape, she could not sleep until morning and just took a shower and went to university. When she got back, she started avoiding him, which was difficult since they were housemates.

She told him that she wasn't happy about what happened, and she had a (long distance) boyfriend to care about. The creep kept stalking, harassing, crying and playing all sorts of tricks on her until she gave up. At one point she spent the night hiding in her office in the university because she was too scared to return home and face the rapist. At another point she even complained to the police and got a restraining order. He played it strategically. He got her fired from her job, her anxiety and panic attacks sent her health spiralling into a disaster of chronic illness, and her long distance boyfriend left her. She was homeless, jobless and penniless. A perfect opportunity for the predator.

He became her boyfriend and guardian, and now the sexual assault was a daily business. The word no never mattered to him anyway. She says that is how the relationship began. Months went by and, because of her deteriorating health condition, she began to see a partner in him. He would take care of her, take her to hospital, pay the bills, do everything that a responsible husband does. Reena doesn't know how to deal with a rapist that pays the bills and takes care of her.

She sees, and admits, that it could be Stockholm Syndrome, but she still has no way out of her situation. She cannot get a job, and being financially independent is a basic survival strategy you need in this very expensive world. She says that one day she will free herself from this prison, but it will be hard. She won't know what part of him to hate and what part to love.

Most importantly, he has total control over her phone, her emails, her social life and everything in between. She is not allowed to talk to a male because, in the words of the guy, "all men are potential rapists and they only want one thing from you".

She feels manic when she hears these words from the mouth of a rapist himself. She displays similar reactions when they watch TV and there is a rape scene or sexual assault; his reaction is unbelievable. He will abuse the rapist and wish the worst kind of painful death upon the rapist or wife abuser. Yet, when he does the exact same thing he is perfectly OK with it. She fails to comprehend how can a man both hate and commit rape.

Maybe this excellent experiment will explain the truth behind the whole confusion. Researchers asked 1,882 men if they had ever held someone down by force or manipulated someone for sex. The exact questions were:

- Have you ever been in a situation where you tried, but for various reasons did not succeed, in having sexual intercourse with an adult by using or threatening to use physical force (twisting their arm, holding them down, etc.) if they did not cooperate?

- Have you ever had sexual intercourse with someone, even though they did not want to, because they were too intoxicated (on alcohol or drugs) to resist your sexual advances (e.g., removing their clothes)?

- Have you ever had sexual intercourse with an adult when they didn't want to because you used or threatened to use physical force (twisting their arm; holding them down, etc.) if they didn't cooperate?

- Have you ever had oral sex with an adult when they didn't want to because you used or threatened to use physical force (twisting their arm; holding them down, etc.) if they didn't cooperate?

Guess what? 120 answered yes. They admitted to 483 rapes. And they were never punished.

The key here is using the language in a way that is descriptive of the action. All the four questions above are descriptions of rape. Yet when you ask a rapist if he is one, he will say no. Men only see rape when they are not the rapist.

The same thing happens in cases of domestic abuse. Men beat and humiliate their wives their entire lives, yet when their daughters get married, they become super sensitive and totally against oppressing women. They very conveniently forget that the woman they have harassed most also had a father, who died a little inside every time he saw a bruise on his daughters face, or a tear in her eye. That was your gift to our wife's family, and it's impossible to return it.

Men will make fun of the stereotype that even God does not know what women want, and how fed up they are trying to understand women. But it's pretty simple actually.

- Ask us how our day was.

- Take an interest in our lives.

- Offer to share household responsibilities, because you fucking live there too.

That's all! Trust me, if men did these three things, us women don't even complain about dying romance and shit because we are smarter than you give us credit for. No matter how many roses you bring or diamonds you buy, if you do not do these above things, the relationship will pretty much stink.

Alas, the moment you say this to a man, he will interrupt you before you finish and mansplain how he just, "can't get what you nagging women want" and, "there is just no pleasing you."

Men will blame women for being too emotional, yet conveniently skip the part where they just cried after their team lost a game in the World Cup Finals.

Take a man like Steve Jobs. Insulting people at work is the behaviour of a serious businessman and a genius, but a woman being just as serious is rude and a bitch.

Brooding men are sexy and taken seriously. Women have a 'resting bitch face'.

Wow, I am too exhausted to point out more hypocrisies and ironies.

Open your eyes people. Open your eyes.

PS. In case you wanted to see the research, the first was a 2002 study done by David Lisak and Paul M. Miller entitled, *"College Men: Repeat Rape and Multiple Offenders Among Undetected Rapists"*. The second was a 2009 study by Stephanie K. McWhorter et al in which the results of the L&M study were duplicated on a larger scale, entitled, *"Reports of Rape Reperpetration by Newly Enlisted Male Navy Personnel"*.

Chapter 14

━━━━━•◦✈◦•━━━━━

Dear White People

Kudos to you if you're reading a book written by, and about, a brown woman. Our voices rarely receive such an honour in the public arena so, first of all, thank you for that.

That being said, don't worry – this is not going to be a rant about how all white people are racist and should learn to embrace diversity. It's about the things I want you to know about us brown women that many people remain ignorant of, often through no fault of their own.

The experiences that us brown – especially immigrant – women go through, and how they make us feel. Maybe, just maybe, learning these things will help you understand us better, and empathise with us if you don't already. Mainly how, when your fight is against sexism, ours is both against racist-sexism and sexist-racism. If you refuse to be open minded enough to step into the third world and be objective and undefensive about things, this may very well seem like a rant. Either way, you might be about to enter a new world, so strap on your seatbelts.

I want you to know that the colour brown is the most boring of *all* colours. I don't own one item of clothing that is brown in my closet. Yet somehow, brown women are *not* boring. Not even a little bit. Our lives are filled with stories that will blow you away; indeed, this book was filled with several so you could get a perspective of how our lives are. You can certainly see a whole lot of oppression and sadness, but the fact that the author of this book is a brown woman must give you a sense of relief. At least there are *some* of us refusing to be silenced, and sharing our tales with the world.

I want you to know that as much as the western world blames alcohol and drugs as the cause of rape and sexual abuse, that's just stupid. In our country, except for the urban, wealthy women, most middle class girls (including myself) cannot tell the difference between vodka and whisky. All the same, rape and sexual assault incidents in our world are excessive. Alcohol is most certainly not to blame; it's always the *rapist* who decides to use a woman's body to dominate his power, and when it comes to rape, it doesn't *matter* how many times you have had sex before, how sexual you are as a woman, or whether your skin is white, brown or black. In every country, to women of every colour, rape feels the same colour – a unique and regrettable shade of pain and horror.

I also want you to know that, while a white woman may *seem* to have a lot of privileges when it comes to her social life, you can never assume that she doesn't need help. Due to the alarming patriarchal norms, people stereotype all brown women as victims of oppression. In some cases, this may not be the case. But when a white woman talks about a violent marriage or abusive relationship, most people wonder why doesn't she just *say something,* or speak up and leave. She knows the language; she is educated; she earns her own money – why does she need help? The fact again is that, in every country, to women of every colour, abuse feels the same colour – an absence of love and belonging.

I want you to know that our childhood was quite similar to yours – except when it wasn't. Many of you share tales of how your first period was celebrated, and you received gifts to start the chapter of womanhood. In my life it was devastating, because our mothers started to treat us as sexual objects, talking to us as though we were open invitations for men. They tried constantly to cover us up, shaming us in the process. Your bedtime stories were about Cinderella and Snow White; ours were about being disciplined wives. Now that I compare the two, I don't feel they are too different at all. In every country, to girls of every colour, future feels the same colour – being an enabler to a man's life.

I want you to know that I love your beautiful skin. During summers, in dusky, long British evenings, as I sit in the garden and observe. I adore your milky white flesh peeking through your revealing clothes. Seeing your lovely legs in shorts or mini skirts, or your glowing arms in a sleeveless top or your daring rebellious back smiling at me through a backless dress... I look at you, and just adore how beautiful you white women are, and how wonderful and liberating it is to see you in your natural habitat. Laughing, strolling, working, feeding, doing everything us brown women dream of. Trust me I don't say that out of envy; you'll find out why soon enough. I see you, and then I see me. If I wore those shorts, the moral policeman that my mom planted inside my head would make me so uncomfortable, I'd dare not step out of the door. And through the lens of that policeman, my arms are gross and so are my legs. I'd love them in my bathtub, but I couldn't *possibly* go out in public to show that love. That's years of white supremacy taught to my people by colonialism, and now engraved in my brain so fiercely. Instead of being self-righteous here, I will admit this is generally the work of an internalised brown inferiority complex and personal insecurity, and I've been working on it for years. Yet I am human. And so are you, which is why I see you buying cans of tanning lotions, and visiting tanning salons. I guess, in every country, to women of every colour, beauty feels the same colour – insecurity.

We are all different, yet the same. And the same, yet different.

Brown women are, in no aspect, inferior or superior to white, black, yellow or blue women.

We are all individuals with our own set of baggage.

Yet the world that is the third one is a lot more hostile to us women. Soon, I'll briefly delve into the historical oppression that all people of colour share.

I could easily be shot dead for writing this book, as it clearly goes against many things the extremists don't want women to discuss openly in the third world. But, since at the moment I am in the first world, I can dare to write and share all this with anybody who may be interested. Hence, this is a privilege that I identify as a woman of colour; a privilege you were born, with but may not see it.

- When you have your first kiss, or bring your first boyfriend home, your parents may not ground you forever, have you married against your will, or straight up shoot you in the head for shaming the family [honour killings and forced marriages].

- When you wear the dress I wear traditionally, (salwar kameez or saree), you might get all sorts of compliments and praise for accepting my culture. But wearing my own cultural attire, I get looked down upon or straight up bullied for the same [Cultural appropriation].

- When you hold your boyfriends' hand on an elevator, or kiss him publically on a moving bus, I cannot help but look at the beauty of human affection that you share. While in my culture a woman inside her own bedroom is slut shamed by her husband for her desires [internalised misogyny].

- I love that when you and your boyfriend decide to live together, with or without getting married first, it's not your father who is forced to pay for every single thing from the furniture to the last piece of clothing or transport [dowry custom].

- I know you get paid less than men at work – but it's still more than us. I think you've already gotten bored of seeing the numbers after Patricia Arquette's Oscar speech and repeating here would be useless [wage inequality within female demographic].

I digress. When I see my life stuck still between visa applications and job rejection letters but still celebrate my white counterparts who started their PhDs with me, who have now graduated, married and became mothers. I do wonder how much money I could have saved if I had their white privileges and how far along my life would be by now.

I feel worthless when I get interviewed for a Masters level position by a white woman that holds a Certificate in Swimming, while me holding an almost completed doctoral candidature. Guess what? I still get rejected because I have not struggled enough yet to be granted the rights of a regular citizen despite paying thrice the sum of fees the local students do. And just so you know, the job was not that of a swim coach.

Migration? Rules? Foreign policy? Call it whatever makes you most comfortable, but it *is* a privilege at the end of the day. A privilege for you, and for which I have dedicated the last eight years of my life and still haven't received the same recognition from. Is it right of me, an immigrant brown woman, to expect the rights and privileges of a settled person? I don't know. Maybe the better question is, "is it right for me to expect to gain a little piece of life as a migrant woman in a country that colonized my own for 200 years, leaving us bankrupt, starving and divided?"

An excellent Indian Politician (this is the second time you will hear me speak positive about a politician, the first one is Justin Trudeau) Dr. Shashi Tharoor took us down the memory lane in his famous Oxford Speech, "*Does Britain Owe India Reparations?*" Here are some excerpts that need echoing, because nobody could have said it better than Dr Tharoor...

India's share of the world economy when Britain arrived on the shores was 23%.

By the time the British had left, it was down to below 4%. Why?

Simply because India had been governed for the benefit of Britain.

In Britain's rise for 200 years was financed by its depredation in India. In fact Britain's industrial revolution was actually permits upon deemed industrialization of India.

The handloom weavers for example – famed across the world, whose products were exported around the world, Britain came right in. There were actually these weavers making fine Muslin, light as woven air it was said, and Britain came in and smashed their thumbs, broke their looms, imposed tariffs and duties on their cloth and products, and started, of course, taking the raw materials in India, and shipping back manufactured cloth, flooding the worlds market with what became the products deemed dark and satanic mills of Victorian England. That meant that the weavers in India became beggars, and India went from being a world famous exporter of finished cloth to an importer. Went from having 27% of world trade to less than 2%.

England on the perceive of their loot in India, while taking the Hindi word loot into their dictionary's as well as their habits, and the British had the gall to call him Clive of India as if he belonged to the country, when all he really did was to ensure that but all the country belonged to him. By the end of the nineteenth century the fact is that India was already Britain's biggest cash cow, the Wolds biggest purchaser of British goods and exports, and the source of highly paid employment for British civil servants.

We literally paid for our own oppression, and as this has been pointed out the worldly Victorian family's that made their money *out of the slave economy, one fifth of the elite, of the wealth class of Britain in the nineteenth century, owed their money to transporting 3 million Africans across the waters. In fact in 1833, when slavery was abolished what happened was that a compensation of 20 million pounds was paid; not as reparations to those who had lost their lives or who had suffered by being oppressed by slavery, <u>but to those who had lost their property.</u>*

I was struck by the fact that the Wi-Fi password of this union commemorates that even Mister Gladstone, great liberal hero. Well I'm sorry, but his family was one of those who benefited from the infamous tragedy. Staying with India, between 15 and 29 million Indians died of starvation in British induced famines.

The most famous example, of course, was the great Bengal famine in the second world war, when 4 million people died because Winston Churchill deliberately – as a matter of written military policy – proceeded to divert essential supply from civilians in Bengal, to sturdy Tommy's and Europeans as reserve stockpiles.

He said that the starvation of any underfed Bengalis mattered much less than that of sturdy Greek sources. Churchill's actual quote, and when conscious stricken British officials wrote to him, pointing out that people were dying because of this decision he peevishly wrote in the margins of the file, "why hasn't Ghandi died yet?"

So all notions that the British were trying to do their colonial enterprise out of enlightened desperation, to try and bring the benefits of colonialism and civilization to the benighted heathen, I'm sorry Churchill's conduct in 1943 is simply one example of many that gave a lie to this myth.

As others have said and done the proposition, violence and racism were the reality of the colonialist experience, and <u>no wonder the sun never set on the British Empire</u> because even God couldn't trust the English in the dark.

Let me take WWI as a very concrete example. Where first speaker Mister Lee suggested these things couldn't be quantified. Well let me quantify WWI for you.

Again I'm sorry for the Indian perspective, others have spoken about the countries.

One sixth of all the British forces that fought in the war were Indian. 54,000 Indians actually lost their lives in that war. 65,000 were wounded. Another 4,000 remained missing or in prison.

Indian taxpayers had to cough up 100 million pounds in that times money.

India supplied 70 million rounds of ammunitions. 600,000 rifles and machine guns. 42 million garments was stitched and sent out of India and 1.3 million Indian personal served in this war.

I know this because, of course, the commemoration of the century has just taken place, but not just that India had to supply 173,000 animals, 370 million tonnes of supplies and in the end the total value of everything that was taken out of India. India, by the way, was suffering from recession at that time, and poverty and hunger was – in today's money – 8 billion pounds.

You want quantification it's available. WWII it was even worse, with two and a half million Indians in uniform.

I won't belabour the point, but of Britain's total war debt of 3 billion pounds in 1945 money, 1.25 billion was owed to India and never actually paid.

Somebody mentioned Scotland. Well, the fact is that colonialism actually cemented your union with Scotland. You know the Scots had actually tried to send colonies out before 1707 and it all failed, I'm sorry to say. But then of course came unions, and India was available, and there you had a disproportionate employment of Scots. I'm sorry Mister McKenzie has to speak after me. In this colonial enterprise as soldiers, as merchants, as agents, as employees and their earnings from India is what brought prosperity to Scotland, even pulled Scotland out of poverty. Now that India is no longer there, no wonder the bonds are loosening.

There has been a mention of the railways. Well let me tell you first of all as my colleague the Jamaican high commissioner pointed out, our railways and roads were really built to serve British interest and not those of the local people. I might add that many countries of railways and roads <u>without having to be colonized in order to do so</u>, they were designed to carry raw materials form into the ports to be shipped to Britain, and the fact is that the Indian or Jamaican or other communion public, their needs were incidental.

Transportation, there was no intent made to match supply to demand from that transport. None whatsoever. Instead, in fact, the Indian railways were built with massive incentives offered by Britain to British investors. Guaranteed out of Indian taxes paid by Indians, with the result that actually had one mile of Indian railway costing twice what it cost to build the same mile in Canada or Australia, because there was so much money being paid in extravagant returns. Britain made all the profits, controlled the technologies, supplied all the equipment, and absolutely all these benefits came as private enterprise. British private enterprise at public risk – Indian public risk.

That was the railways as an accomplishment.

We are hearing about aid, I think it was again Sir Richard mentioned British aid to India. Well let me just point out that British aid to India is about 0.4% of India's GDP. The government of India actually spends more on fertilizer subsidies, which might be an appropriate metaphor for that argument.

If I may point out as well that as my fellow speaker's proposition had pointed out, there had been incidents of racial violence and looting, massacres and bloodshed, of transportation.

In India's case even one of our last Mughal emperor. Yes maybe todays Britain's aren't responsible for some of these reparations, but he same speakers have pointed with pride to their foreign aid.

You are not responsible for the people starving in Somalia but you give the aid, surely the principle of reparations for what is for the wrongs that have been done cannot be denied.

It's been pointed out, for example, the dehumanization of Africans in the Caribbean, the massive physiological damage that has been done. The undermining of social traditions of property rights, of the authority structures of these societies all in the interest of professional colonialism. The fact remains that many of today's problems in these countries, including the persistence and in some cases the creation of, racial and ethnic and religious tensions were the direct result of the colonial experience. So there is a moral debt that needs to be paid. Someone challenged reparations elsewhere.

Well, I'm sorry, Germany doesn't just give reparations to Israel. It also gave reparation to Poland. Perhaps some of the speakers here are too young to remember the dramatic picture of Chancellor Willie Brown on his knees in the Walto ghetto in 1970, and there are other examples. There are Italia's reparations to Libya. There is Japan's to Korea. Even Britain has paid reparation to the New Zealand Maoris. So it's not as though this is something unprecedented and unheard of; that is going to somehow open a nasty Pandora 's Box. No wonder professor Louis reminded us that he is from Texas. There is a wonderful expression in Texas that summarizes the arguments of the oppositions; all hat and not cattle.

Let me say with the greatest possible respect, you cannot be rich to oppressed, enslaved, killed, torture, name people for 200 years and then celebrate the fact that they are democratic at the end of it. We were denied democracies so we had to snatch it, seize it from you.

Certainly no amount of money can be at the loss of a loved one as somebody pointed out there.

You are not going to be able to figure out the exact amount, but the principle is what matters. The fact is that to speak blindly of sacrifices on both sides as an analogy was used here, <u>a burglar comes into your house, ransacks the place, stubs his toe and you say he was a sacrifice on both sides.</u> That I'm sorry to say is not an acceptable. It is not an acceptable argument.

The truth is that we are not arguing specifically that vast sums of money need to be paid. The proposition for this house is the principle of owing reparations, not the fine points of how much is owed to whom it should be paid. **The question is there a debt.**

Does Britain owe reparations? As far as I'm concerned, the ability to acknowledge a wrong that has been done, to simply say <u>sorry</u>, will go far, far, far further than some percentage of GDP in the form of aid. What is required seems to me is accepting the principle that reparations are owed. Personally, I would be quite happy if it was 1 pound a year for the next 200 years after the last 200 years of Britain and India.

Sorry if Dr. Tharoor's speech has left a bitter taste in your mouth about colonized people, but what we see around today has been built on this very history.

As Indians of this generation, we are tremendously happy to come to the UK, learn your language, learn your life ways, assimilate totally into your world until we only find slight shreds of ours left in some corners of our now migrated memories.

We love you. We respect that your nations are advanced and progressive.

So many of us want to be part of that progressive new first world because ours is still too busy deciding if beef or mutton should be banned. Hence, we travel. We leave behind our beloved families and friends and in search of a better life we come to the first world.

When you see us, please don't assume we all come from the same beginnings, because we are too many to be stereotyped as a singular entity.

Keep in mind that, due to our skin colour, we may or may not be discriminated against at some point, even if we were born in the first world. So please don't say things like, "I don't see colour".

At work, speaking panels, conferences, meetings, art competitions, music, cinema, any other platform, please be mindful of your privileges and the experiences that other non-whites may bring along, just like Adele towards Beyoncé.

I was once lecturing an undergraduate session for Bachelor of Business Admin students where the entire class was Caucasian except for one refugee guy from the Middle East. Every discussion we had in the classroom, somehow he dragged the topic to the war and politics going on in Afghanistan.

I observed him few times and once sat down with him after class. I asked where was he from and his background etc.

He said he saw his family blow up before his very eyes when he was 14, and now he is a refugee in the UK. I could barely hold in my tears while I listened to his agony. Once he stopped, I asked if he had any friends. He said he had some outside class, but none here.

That's when I told him – with no judgment and no preaching – that I been through the same experience. Of course, not the war part, but of *isolation*. At some point I made it relatable, and made him comfortable enough to put down the defensive shields that appeared to surround him.

I explained that we are the ones that come from another world, and the majority of the people here have not seen that. Hence, to expect them to understand your world, or be able to discuss war and politics from your perspective, is not going to help. We all come from diverse circumstances and the best we can do is to get to know each other, and that may not happen if your defence shield is always up. His classmates were not racist, but he was too timid to even give them a shot.

To make friends, you need to give them a chance. And to give them a chance, you have to find something relatable, something you have in common with them. It could be as simple as this class. Once in class, you can introduce yourself, talk to people who sit right beside you, and slowly start hanging out with people you feel comfortable with.

The advice worked, and just two sessions later I found him in the cafeteria with a bunch of his new white friends.

This is what he did, what I did, and what every person does when they are in the vicinity of white people, or that of other colours than him or her.

So, dear white women, your privilege and oppression follow you like two shadows caused by your white body. I see your privileges as they are missing in my life. I see your oppression because I've got it worse. My share of sexism is often racial and my share of racism is also sexualised.

I only wish that you could see it too. My oppression, my privilege, and my truth.

"The truth is hard.

The truth is hidden.

The truth must be pursued.

The truth is hard to hear.

The truth is rarely simple.

The truth isn't so obvious.

The truth is necessary.

The truth can't be glossed over.

The truth has no agenda.

The can't be manufactured.

The truth doesn't take sides.

The truth isn't red or blue.

The truth is hard to accept.

The truth pulls no punches.

The truth is powerful.

The truth is under attack.

The truth is worth defending.

The truth requires taking a stand.

The truth is more important now than ever."

- The New York Times

The question now is what are you going to do with this truth?

No, I don't want you to be my saviour. I don't want you to fight my oppression for me. Just start by identifying your privileges. If you cant see any, try *way* harder, because this book must have failed in its mission if you didn't see your privileges yet.

With brown love,

Shahla (that means the brightest star in the sky! Clearly my parents had bigger hopes for me but what can I do, I ended up being the sun that burns misogynists.)

XX

PS. Chicken Tikka is not the only thing attractive about brown people. If you haven't tried Biryani yet, you're certainly missing out in life!

AFTERWORD

Like every burning romance and magnificent sunset, this book has now come to its conclusion. The stories have been told and rants have been shared. Yet, this is not the end. As I mentioned in chapter 1, a feminist's work is never complete.

Whether you identify as a feminist or not (although, I hope you do), I am sure there must be something about this book that convinced you to read this far. If it's hatred, please keep it to yourself – the world has enough of that already. If you related to something you have read, let me know what it was. If you think any part of this book can help open the widely closed eyes of somebody, kindly share the book with them.

And most of all, if you liked it, please leave a review on Amazon as I would love to read your thoughts and have others know what you liked about this book.

In case you wanted to see me LIVE, talking, walking, ranting and sometimes dancing, I have a YouTube channel called Womanlyyy where I talk about empowering women's financial, emotional and physical powers. You are most welcome to check it out and stay connected with me, despite the ending of this book.

The seed of the idea to write this book was planted in my mind in 2014. I had a different title in mind, but the idea was to compile a whole bunch of real life stories that I found appalling and repulsive. I wanted to share them with my readers because, let's face it; the longer we hide, the more power we give to the idiots of this world. People who think women are still in the stone ages, unaware of the difference between right and wrong. With this book, I wanted to mock patriarchy and call out those that oppress women.

Few stories have been told. Millions wait to be told. My mission to share the ones that impacted upon me personally to date is almost over. It is safe to say I spent the last three years writing, rewriting and adding to these weird AF incidents. It is sad that these things happened to these women, yet it is a relief that I could document them and recognise these atrocities.

The third world certainly seems way shittier, but there is a lot of work still to be done in the first world – especially now specifically in America, where everything from abortion rights to women's safety is at risk. Britain has been struggling with its own issues around domestic violence, extremism, funding cuts and austerity. Russia literally constructed Nazi-like camps to torture and kill gays while decriminalising (some forms of) domestic violence. Australia does not lag behind, with high rates of violence against women; almost one in three Australian women experience physical violence, and almost one in five women experience sexual violence in their lifetime. Aboriginal and Torres Strait Islander women experience horrific levels of violence, and are 35 times more likely to be hospitalised as a result of spousal or partner violence than non-Indigenous women. I had better hopes for Japan, but it turns out that women's participation in their national workforce is meagre, and their wages and working conditions require a lot of improvement. Also, Japan tops the unwelcome chart for exploitation of schoolgirls, with the multimillion-pound porn industry forcing many to commit suicide.

No country is perfect but certainly Sweden, Norway, Canada and Netherlands are leading the way in many areas. I personally have not been to either of these countries nor do I have a friend from there but I hope to visit someday and talk at length about their stories. How vastly different would their lives be from mine and just for a moment, imagine what its like to be without rules.

Anger made me write this book because I wanted to channel my feelings when I read and hear of such assaults on women. While anger is usually considered a negative emotion, I see it as a motivation. I don't *want* to remain calm when I see humans being killed, tortured and maimed. Peace has its merits, I know, but if I have learned anything while writing this book is that if your blood does not boil seeing others oppressed and if you have accepted oppression without question, staying peaceful is slow poison.

Imagine how many million tiny little cells of sperm crawled towards your mom's embryo, and it was *you* that was given the chance of survival. That fighting chance to form a human foetus and beating pulse. What were the odds of you not being alive? Millions! And you *beat* those odds. Literally, you are one in a million.

To be one in a million and let go of your rights to live the way you want is such a waste. I write books, blogs and make videos on feminism and female empowerment, despite never actually taking a single class in gender studies or psychology and healing. Everything I know is self-taught. And it's now easier than ever with such awesome technology on our side.

My closing message to you is this – speak out, stand for, get angry, be outraged, and rant at the top of your lungs against any injustice of your choice. Choose whatever medium you can, whatever time you can, but do it.

The happiest I have ever felt about my existence is when a stranger from miles away writes to me only to thank me for inspiring them to believe in themselves. You never know whose life you may impact, and who could live a day more because of you.

Keep up the good fight, my dear. You will always find me by your side.

Illustration/image credits – Photographs and images with attribution and copyright noted.

About the Author

Shahla Khan is hell bent upon making this world a little more feminist through her efforts as an author, blogger, YouTuber and now as a filmmaker too. She speaks at educational institutions to educate students and faculties about gender equality, consent, workplace harassment and women's rights. Miss Khan empowers her fans to achieve their professional goals as well as ways to make happy and healthy relationships. Turns out there are a lot of unhappy couples out there.

Her book *Lean On What* was an award-winning take on how women are mistreated in tech industries. Her blend of Asian and Muslim cultures tangled with her European education makes her a perfect concoction of ideologies and conflicts.

Professionally she completed her MBA in International Business at Kurt Bosch University in Switzerland and continued to pursue her Ph.D. in Corporate Learning in the UK. She has not undertaken feminist theory as an academic subject ever. Yet when she began her research on women's rights, she explored self-learning to a new level. She achieved distinction in her courses; Understanding Violence from Emory University, Human Trafficking from The Ohio State University and Women in Leadership from The Case Western University, thanks to Coursera.

She also devoured several books in her research before she became a feminist author. She also makes regular radio appearances and provides workshops and training on inclusion and diversity. Miss Khan's mission in life is to heal and empower other women who've been oppressed by the notions of patriarchy. She helps her blog readers and YouTube audiences by providing them with an opportunity to interact with her directly about their issues. She provides them educational resources and guidance and suggests therapy where necessary, all free of charge.

Miss Khan is a total night owl as it enables her creativity. She is deeply inspired by Virginia Woolf's *A Room Of One's Own* which led her to create her own special little space she calls **The Warrior's Den**. A cozy yet highly efficient workspace where all her creative ambitions turn from dream to reality. One of her most important messages to her viewers is for women to attain financial independence so they can live a life of dignity without compromising and settling for the wrong kind of men in their lives.

Miss Khan's upcoming books are *Perks of Being Single* and a feminist Comic book based on real-life stories of Indian women she knows. Keep in touch with her on her website and social media channels to be updated about her work.

Check her out on :

Facebook www.facebook.com/Womanlyyy/

Twitter @ShahlaSparkle

YouTube http://bit.ly/2zH5x67

Website www.shahlakhan.me

Blog That Feminist Life https://authorshahla.wordpress.com/